# › SPSS® 13.0 Brief Guide

AUTHORIZATION CODE

632a56E444E867Od7918

For more information about SPSS® software products, please visit our Web site at *http://www.spss.com* or contact

SPSS Inc.
233 South Wacker Drive, 11th Floor
Chicago, IL 60606-6412
Tel: (312) 651-3000
Fax: (312) 651-3668

# *Preface*

The *SPSS® 13.0 Brief Guide* provides a set of tutorials designed to acquaint you with the various components of the SPSS system. You can work through the tutorials in sequence or turn to the topics for which you need additional information. You can use this guide as a supplement to the online tutorial that is included with the SPSS Base 13.0 system or ignore the online tutorial and start with the tutorials found here.

## *SPSS 13.0*

SPSS 13.0 is a comprehensive system for analyzing data. SPSS can take data from almost any type of file and use them to generate tabulated reports, charts, and plots of distributions and trends, descriptive statistics, and complex statistical analyses.

SPSS makes statistical analysis more accessible for the beginner and more convenient for the experienced user. Simple menus and dialog box selections make it possible to perform complex analyses without typing a single line of command syntax. The Data Editor offers a simple and efficient spreadsheet-like facility for entering data and browsing the working data file.

### *Internet Resources*

The SPSS Web site (*http://www.spss.com*) offers answers to frequently asked questions about installing and running SPSS software and provides access to data files and other useful information.

In addition, the SPSS USENET discussion group (not sponsored by SPSS) is open to anyone interested in SPSS products. The USENET address is *comp.soft-sys.stat.spss*. It deals with computer, statistical, and other operational issues related to SPSS software.

You can also subscribe to an e-mail message list that is gatewayed to the USENET group. To subscribe, send an e-mail message to *listserv@listserv.uga.edu*. The text of the e-mail message should be: subscribe SPSSX-L firstname lastname. You can then post messages to the list by sending an e-mail message to *listserv@listserv.uga.edu*.

## Additional Publications

For additional information about the features and operations of SPSS Base 13.0, you can consult the *SPSS Base 13.0 User's Guide*, which includes information on standard graphics. Examples using the statistical procedures found in SPSS Base 13.0 are provided in the Help system, installed with the software. Algorithms used in the statistical procedures are available on the product CD-ROM.

In addition, beneath the menus and dialog boxes, SPSS uses a command language. Some extended features of the system can be accessed only via command syntax. (Those features are not available in the Student Version.) Complete command syntax is documented in the *SPSS 13.0 Command Syntax Reference*, available in PDF form from the Help menu.

Individuals worldwide can order additional product manuals directly from SPSS Inc. For telephone orders in the United States and Canada, call SPSS Inc. at 800-543-2185. For telephone orders outside of North America, contact your local office, listed on the SPSS Web site at *http://www.spss.com/worldwide*.

The *SPSS Statistical Procedures Companion*, by Marija Norušis, has been published by Prentice Hall. It contains overviews of the procedures in the SPSS Base, plus Logistic Regression and General Linear Models. A *Statistical Procedures Companion* covering advanced procedures is forthcoming.

## SPSS Options

The following options are available as add-on enhancements to the full (not Student Version) SPSS Base system:

**SPSS Regression Models™** provides techniques for analyzing data that do not fit traditional linear statistical models. It includes procedures for probit analysis, logistic regression, weight estimation, two-stage least-squares regression, and general nonlinear regression.

**SPSS Advanced Models™** focuses on techniques often used in sophisticated experimental and biomedical research. It includes procedures for general linear models (GLM), linear mixed models, variance components analysis, loglinear analysis, ordinal regression, actuarial life tables, Kaplan-Meier survival analysis, and basic and extended Cox regression.

**SPSS Tables™** creates a variety of presentation-quality tabular reports, including complex stub-and-banner tables and displays of multiple response data.

**SPSS Trends™** performs comprehensive forecasting and time series analyses with multiple curve-fitting models, smoothing models, and methods for estimating autoregressive functions.

**SPSS Categories®** performs optimal scaling procedures, including correspondence analysis.

**SPSS Conjoint™** performs conjoint analysis.

**SPSS Exact Tests™** calculates exact $p$ values for statistical tests when small or very unevenly distributed samples could make the usual tests inaccurate.

**SPSS Missing Value Analysis™** describes patterns of missing data, estimates means and other statistics, and imputes values for missing observations.

**SPSS Maps™** turns your geographically distributed data into high-quality maps with symbols, colors, bar charts, pie charts, and combinations of themes to present not only what is happening but where it is happening.

**SPSS Complex Samples™** allows survey, market, health, and public opinion researchers, as well as social scientists who use sample survey methodology, to incorporate their complex sample designs into data analysis.

**SPSS Classification Tree™** creates a tree-based classification model. It classifies cases into groups or predicts values of a dependent (target) variable based on values of independent (predictor) variables. The procedure provides validation tools for exploratory and confirmatory classification analysis.

The SPSS family of products also includes applications for data entry, text analysis, classification, neural networks, and flowcharting.

### Training Seminars

SPSS Inc. provides both public and onsite training seminars for SPSS. All seminars feature hands-on workshops. SPSS seminars will be offered in major U.S. and European cities on a regular basis. For more information on these seminars, contact your local office, listed on the SPSS Web site at *http://www.spss.com/worldwide*.

### Technical Support

The services of SPSS Technical Support are available to registered customers of SPSS. (Student Version customers should read the special section on technical support for the Student Version. For more information, see "Technical Support for Students" on p. vii.) Customers may contact Technical Support for assistance in using SPSS products or for installation help for one of the supported hardware environments. To reach Technical Support, see the SPSS Web site at *http://www.spss.com*, or contact your local office, listed on the SPSS Web site at *http://www.spss.com/worldwide*. Be prepared to identify yourself, your organization, and the serial number of your system.

### Tell Us Your Thoughts

Your comments are important. Please let us know about your experiences with SPSS products. We especially like to hear about new and interesting applications using the SPSS system. Please send e-mail to *suggest@spss.com*, or write to SPSS Inc., Attn: Director of Product Planning, 233 South Wacker Drive, 11th Floor, Chicago IL 60606-6412.

## SPSS 13.0 for Windows Student Version

The SPSS 13.0 for Windows Student Version is a limited but still powerful version of the SPSS Base 13.0 system.

### Capability

The Student Version contains all of the important data analysis tools contained in the full SPSS Base system, including:

■ Spreadsheet-like Data Editor for entering, modifying, and viewing data files.

- Statistical procedures, including *t* tests, analysis of variance, and crosstabulations.
- Interactive graphics that allow you to change or add chart elements and variables dynamically; the changes appear as soon as they are specified.
- Standard high-resolution graphics for an extensive array of analytical and presentation charts and tables.

## Limitations

Created for classroom instruction, the Student Version is limited to use by students and instructors for educational purposes only. The Student Version does not contain all of the functions of the SPSS Base 13.0 system. The following limitations apply to the SPSS 13.0 for Windows Student Version:

- Data files cannot contain more than 50 variables.
- Data files cannot contain more than 1,500 cases. SPSS add-on modules (such as Regression Models or Advanced Models) cannot be used with the Student Version.
- SPSS command syntax is not available to the user. This means that it is not possible to repeat an analysis by saving a series of commands in a syntax or "job" file, as can be done in the full version of SPSS.
- Scripting and automation are not available to the user. This means that you cannot create scripts that automate tasks that you repeat often, as can be done in the full version of SPSS.

## Technical Support for Students

Students should obtain technical support from their instructors or from local support staff identified by their instructors. Technical support from SPSS for the SPSS 13.0 Student Version is provided *only to instructors using the system for classroom instruction.*

Before seeking assistance from your instructor, please write down the information described below. Without this information, your instructor may be unable to assist you:

- The type of PC you are using, as well as the amount of RAM and free disk space you have.
- The operating system of your PC.

- A clear description of what happened and what you were doing when the problem occurred. If possible, please try to reproduce the problem with one of the sample data files provided with the program.

- The exact wording of any error or warning messages that appeared on your screen.

- How you tried to solve the problem on your own.

### Technical Support for Instructors

Instructors using the Student Version for classroom instruction may contact SPSS Technical Support for assistance. In the United States and Canada, call SPSS Technical Support at 312-651-3410, or send an e-mail to *support@spss.com*. Please include your name, title, and academic institution.

Instructors outside of the United States and Canada should contact your local SPSS office, listed on the SPSS Web site at *http://www.spss.com/worldwide*.

# Contents

# 4   *Using the Data Editor*     *51*

# 5   *Examining Summary Statistics for Individual Variables*     *79*

# 6 Working with Output 89

# 7 Creating and Editing Charts 127

# 8  Working with Syntax                                          171

# 9  Modifying Data Values                                       177

# 10  Sorting and Selecting Data                                 195

# 11 Additional Statistical Procedures 207

# Index 229

# *Introduction*

This guide provides a set of tutorials designed to acquaint you with the various components of the SPSS system. You can work through the tutorials in sequence or turn to the topics for which you need additional information. The goal is to enable you to perform useful analyses on your data using SPSS.

This chapter will introduce you to the basic environment of SPSS and demonstrate a typical session. We will run SPSS, retrieve a previously defined SPSS data file, and then produce a simple statistical summary and a chart. In the process, you will learn the roles of the primary windows within SPSS and will see a few features that smooth the way when you are running analyses.

More detailed instruction about many of the topics touched upon in this chapter will follow in later chapters. Here, we hope to give you a basic framework for understanding and using SPSS.

## *Sample Files*

Most of the examples presented here use the data file *demo.sav*. This data file is a fictitious survey of several thousand people, containing basic demographic and consumer information.

All sample files used in these examples are located in the folder in which SPSS is installed or in the *tutorial\sample_files* folder within the SPSS installation folder.

# Starting SPSS

To start SPSS:

▶ From the Windows Start menu choose:

Programs
  SPSS for Windows
    SPSS for Windows

To start SPSS for Windows Student Version:

▶ From the Windows Start menu choose:

Programs
  SPSS for Windows Student Version

When you start a session, you see the Data Editor window.

Figure 1-1
*Data Editor window (Data View)*

## *Variable Display in Dialog Boxes*

Either variable names or longer variable labels will appear in list boxes in dialog boxes. Additionally, variables in list boxes can be ordered alphabetically or by their position in the file.

In this guide, we will display variable labels in alphabetical order within list boxes. For a new user of SPSS, this provides a more complete description of variables in an easy-to-follow order.

Since the default setting within SPSS is to display variable labels in file order, we will change this before accessing data.

▶ From the menus choose:
Edit
  Options...

▶ Select Display labels in the Variable Lists group on the General tab.

▶ Also select Alphabetical.

▶ Click OK, and then click OK to confirm the change.

# *Opening a Data File*

Before you can analyze data, you need some data to analyze.

To open a data file:

▶ From the menus choose:
File
  Open
    Data...

Alternatively, you can use the Open File button on the toolbar.

**Figure 1-2**
*Open File toolbar button*

This opens the Open File dialog box.

**Figure 1-3**
*Open File dialog box*

By default, SPSS-format data files (*.sav* extension) are displayed. You can display other file formats using the Files of Type drop-down list.

By default, data files in the folder (directory) in which SPSS is installed are displayed. The files for this guide are located in the folder in which SPSS is installed or in the *tutorial\sample_files* folder within the SPSS installation folder.

▶ Double-click the *tutorial* folder.

▶ Double-click the *sample_files* folder.

▶ Click the file *demo.sav* in the files list box (or just *demo* if file extensions are not displayed).

Figure 1-4
*Sample_files folder displayed in Open File dialog box*

▶ Click Open to open the SPSS data file.

Figure 1-5
*Variable labels*

The data file is displayed in the Data Editor. If you put the mouse cursor on a variable name (the column headings), a more descriptive variable label is displayed if one has been defined for that variable.

By default, the actual data values are displayed. To display labels:

▶ From the menus choose:
View
  Value Labels


Alternatively, you can use the Label tool on the toolbar.

Figure 1-6
*Value Labels tool*

Descriptive value labels are now displayed. This makes it easier to interpret the responses.

Figure 1-7
*Value labels displayed in the Data Editor*

| Data Editor |  |  |  |  |  |  |  |
| --- | --- | --- | --- | --- | --- | --- | --- |
| File | Edit | View | Data | Transform | Analyze | Graphs | Utilities Window Help |

| 11 : age | | | 26 | | | |
| --- | --- | --- | --- | --- | --- | --- |
|  | age | marital | address | income | inccat | car |
| 1 | 37 | Married | 12 | 35.00 | $25,00 | 18 |
| 2 | 33 | Married | 12 | 29.00 | $25,00 | 15 |
| 3 | 42 | Married | 21 | 34.00 | $25,00 | 15 |
| 4 | 58 | Unmarried | 28 | 49.00 | $25,00 | 33 |
| 5 | 56 | Unmarried | 9 | 57.00 | $50,00 | 19 |
| 6 | 46 | Unmarried | 5 | 39.00 | $25,00 | 18 |
| 7 | 47 | Married | 4 | 56.00 | $50,00 | 28 |
| 8 | 62 | Married | 16 | 250.00 | $75,00 | 77 |
| 9 | 52 | Married | 27 | 73.00 | $50.00 | 33 |

Data View / Variable View /

# *Running an Analysis*

The Analyze menu contains a list of general reporting and statistical analysis categories. Most of the categories are followed by an arrow, which indicates that there are several analysis procedures available within the category; they will appear on a submenu when the category is selected.

We'll start with a simple frequency table (table of counts).

▶ From the menus choose:

Analyze
  Descriptive Statistics
    Frequencies...

This opens the Frequencies dialog box.

**Figure 1-8**
*Frequencies dialog box*

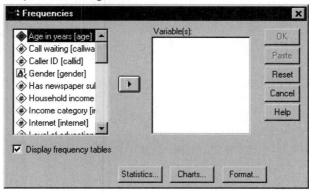

▶ Select (click) the variable *Income category*.

**Figure 1-9**
*Variable labels and names in the Frequencies dialog box*

A more complete description of each variable pops up when the cursor is over it. The variable name (in square brackets) is *inccat*, and it has the variable label *Income category*. If there were no variable label, only the variable name would appear in the list box.

In the dialog box, you choose the variables you want to analyze from the source list on the left and move them into the Variable(s) list on the right. The **OK** button, which runs the analysis, is disabled until at least one variable is placed in the Variable(s) list.

Additional labeling information can be easily obtained for any variable on the list by clicking on the variable name with the right mouse button.

▶ Click the right mouse button on *Income Category [inccat]*, and then click (left mouse button) Variable Information.

▶ Click the down arrow on the Value Labels drop-down list.

Figure 1-10
*Defined labels for income variable*

All of the defined value labels for the variable are displayed.

▶ Click *Gender [gender]* in the source variable list, and then click the right-arrow button to move the variable into the target Variable(s) list.

▶ Click *Income category [inccat]* in the source list, and then click the right arrow button again.

Figure 1-11
*Variables selected for analysis*

A pound sign (#) icon next to the variable name indicates that the variable is **numeric**. An icon with the letter "A" indicates that the variable is a **string** (alphanumeric) variable, which may contain both letters and numbers. A less-than sign (left angle bracket) indicates that the variable is a **short string**, containing eight or fewer characters.

▶ Click OK to run the procedure.

# *Viewing Results*

Figure 1-12
*Viewer window*

Results are displayed in the Viewer window.

You can quickly go to any item in the Viewer simply by selecting it in the outline pane.

▶ Click Income category.

Figure 1-13
*Frequency table of income categories*

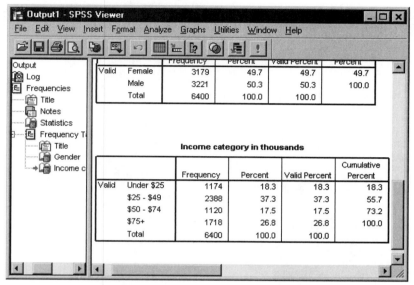

This takes you directly to the frequency table for income categories. This frequency table shows the number and percentage of people in each income category.

# Creating Charts

Although some statistical procedures can create high-resolution charts, you can also use the Graphs menu to create charts.

For example, you could create a chart that shows the relationship between wireless telephone service and PDA (personal digital assistant) ownership.

▶ From the menus choose:
Graphs
  Bar...

▶ Click Clustered and then click Define.

Figure 1-14
*Define Clustered Bar dialog box*

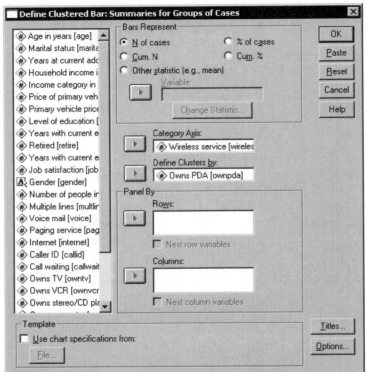

▶ Scroll down the source variable list and select *Wireless service [wireless]* as the Category Axis variable.

▶ Select *Owns PDA [ownpda]* as the Define Clusters By variable.

▶ Click OK to create the chart.

Figure 1-15
*Bar chart displayed in Viewer window*

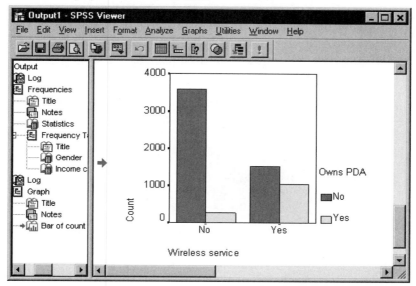

The bar chart is displayed in the Viewer. It shows that people with wireless phone service are far more likely to have PDAs than people without wireless service.

You can edit charts and tables by double-clicking on them in the contents pane of the Viewer window, and you can copy and paste your results into other applications. Those topics will be covered later.

# Exiting SPSS

To exit SPSS:

▶ From the menus choose:
File
  Exit

▶ Click No if you get an alert asking if you want to save your results.

# *Using the Help System*

Help is available in a number of different ways, including:

**Help menu.** Every window has a Help menu on the menu bar. The Topics menu item provides access to the Help system, where you can use the Contents and Index tabs to find topics. The Tutorial menu item provides access to the introductory tutorial.

**Dialog box Help buttons.** Most dialog boxes have a Help button that takes you directly to a Help topic for that dialog box. The Help topic provides general information and links to related topics.

**Pivot table context menu Help.** Right-click on terms in an activated pivot table in the Viewer and select What's This? from the context menu to display definitions of the terms.

**Statistics Coach.** The Statistics Coach item on the Help menu provides a wizard-like method for finding the right statistical or charting procedure for what you want to do.

**Case Studies.** The Case Studies item on the Help menu provides hands-on examples of how to create various types of statistical analyses and interpret the results. The sample data files used in the examples are also provided so that you can work through the examples to see exactly how the results were produced.

This chapter uses the files *demo.sav* and *bhelptut.spo*.

# *Help Contents Tab*

The Topics item on the Help menu opens a Help window.

► From the menus choose:

Help
  Topics

Figure 2-1
*Help Contents tab*

The Contents tab in the left pane of the Help window is an expandable and collapsible table of contents. It is most useful if you're looking for general information or are unsure of what index term to use to find what you're looking for.

# Help Index Tab

Figure 2-2
*Help Index tab*

▶ Click the Index tab in the left pane of the Help window.

The Index tab provides a searchable index that makes it easy to find specific topics. The Index tab is organized in alphabetical order, just like a book index. It uses **incremental search** to find what you're looking for.

For example, you can:

▶ Type med.

**Figure 2-3**
*Incremental index search*

The index scrolls to and highlights the first index entry that starts with these letters, which is median.

# Dialog Box Help

Most dialog boxes have a Help button that displays a Help topic about what the dialog box does and how to do it.

▶ From the menus choose:

Analyze
  Descriptive Statistics
    Frequencies...

▶ Click Help.

Figure 2-4
*Dialog box Help topic*

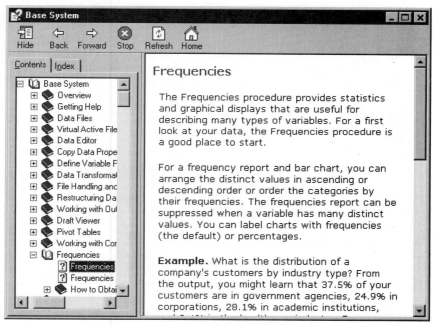

In this example, the Help topic describes the purpose of the Frequencies procedure and provides an example.

## Statistics Coach

The Statistics Coach can help to guide you through the process of finding the procedure that you want to use.

▶ From the menus choose:
Help
  Statistics Coach

Figure 2-5
*Statistics Coach, first step*

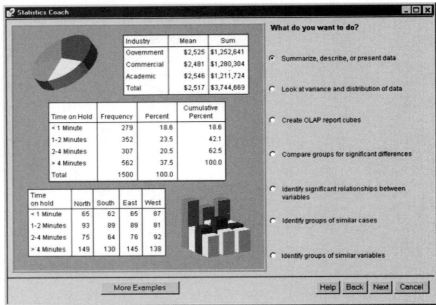

The Statistics Coach presents a series of questions designed to find the appropriate procedure. The first question is simply "What do you want to do?"

For example, if you want to summarize data:

▶ Select Summarize, describe, or present data.

▶ Then click Next.

Figure 2-6
*Data type selection*

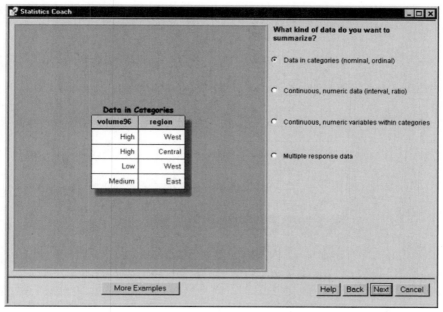

The next question asks about the type of data you want to summarize. If you're unsure, each choice displays different examples.

▶ Select Continuous, numeric data (interval, ratio).

Figure 2-7
*Selecting a different data type*

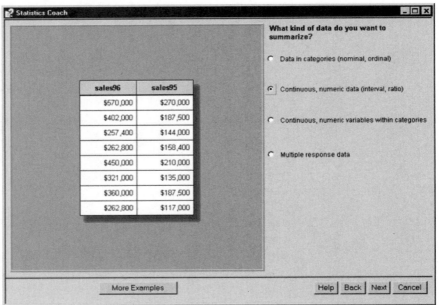

The example changes to reflect your choice. If you're still unsure, you can:

▶ Click More Examples.

A new example of the same data type is displayed. If the examples don't provide enough information, you can:

▶ Click Help.

Figure 2-8
*Statistics Coach Help topic*

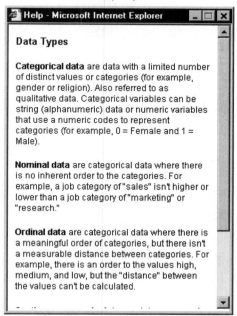

In this example, the Help topic defines the different data types.

▶ Close the Help window.

▶ Select Data in categories (nominal, ordinal) and click Next.

▶ Select Tables and numbers and click Next.

Figure 2-9
*Selecting tables or charts*

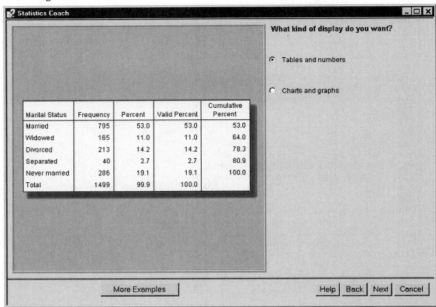

▶ Select Individual case listings within categories.

Figure 2-10
*Statistics Coach, final step*

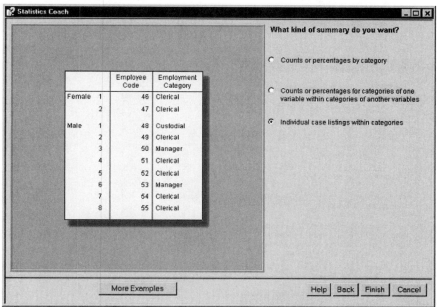

When the Statistics Coach has enough information, the Next button changes to Finish.

When you click Finish, the dialog box for the selected procedure opens automatically, and a Help topic for the procedure is also displayed.

**Figure 2-11**
*Dialog box and Help topic*

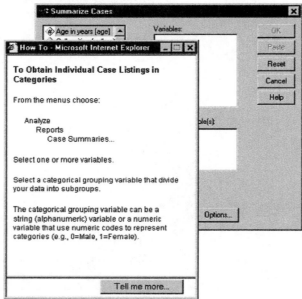

This is a custom Help topic, based on your selections in the Statistics Coach. Since some dialog boxes perform numerous functions, more than one path in the Statistics Coach may lead to the same dialog box, but the instructions in the Help topic may be different.

▶ Click Tell me more in the Help topic to get more detailed information.

Figure 2-12
*"Tell me more" Help topic*

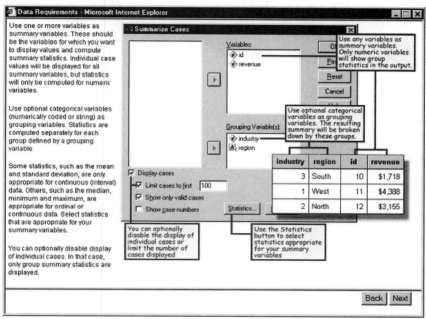

This Help topic provides detailed information on the data type(s) appropriate for the selected procedure.

# Case Studies

Case studies provide comprehensive overviews of each procedure. Data files used in the examples are installed with SPSS, so you can follow along, performing the same analysis—from opening the data source and selecting variables for analysis to interpreting the results.

To access the case studies:

▶ Right-click on any pivot table created by a procedure. For example, you can right-click on the frequency table for Gender.

Figure 2-13
*Accessing the case studies*

▶ Select Case Studies on the pop-up context menu.

Case studies are not available for all procedures. The Case Studies choice on the context menu will appear only if the feature is available for the procedure that created the selected pivot table.

# *Reading Data*

Data can be entered directly into SPSS, or it can be imported from a number
of different sources. The processes for reading data stored in SPSS data files,
spreadsheet applications, such as Microsoft Excel, database applications, such as
Microsoft Access, and text files are all discussed in this chapter.

## *Basic Structure of an SPSS Data File*

Figure 3-1
*Data Editor*

SPSS data files are organized by cases (rows) and variables (columns). In this data
file, cases represent individual respondents to a survey. Variables represent each
question asked in the survey.

# *Reading an SPSS Data File*

SPSS data files, which have a *.sav* file extension, contain your saved data. To open *demo.sav*, an example file that is installed with the product:

▶ From the menus choose:
File
  Open
    Data...

▶ Make sure that SPSS (*.sav) is selected in the Files of Type drop-down list.

Figure 3-2
*Open File dialog box*

▶ Navigate to the *sample_files* folder.

▶ Select *demo.sav* and click Open.

The data are now displayed in the Data Editor.

**Figure 3-3**
*Opened data file*

# Reading Data from Spreadsheets

Rather than typing all of your data directly into the Data Editor, you can read data from applications such as Microsoft Excel. You can also read column headings as variable names.

▶ From the menus choose:
File
  Open
    Data...

▶ Select Excel (*.xls) from the Files of Type drop-down list.

Figure 3-4
*Open File dialog box*

▶ Select *demo.xls* and click Open to read this spreadsheet.

The Opening Excel Data Source dialog box is displayed, allowing you to specify whether variable names are to be included in the spreadsheet, as well as the cells that you want to import. In Excel 5 or later, you can also specify which worksheets you want to import.

Figure 3-5
*Opening Excel Data Source dialog box*

▶ Make sure that Read variable names from first row of data is selected. This option reads column headings as variable names.

If the column headings do not conform to the SPSS variable-naming rules, they are converted into valid variable names and the original column headings are saved as variable labels. If you want to import only a portion of the spreadsheet, specify the range of cells to be imported in the Range text box.

▶ Click OK to read the Excel file.

The data now appear in the Data Editor, with the column headings used as variable names. If you're using a spreadsheet application other than Excel or Lotus, you should be able to export your data to a supported format that can then be read into SPSS.

Figure 3-6
*Imported Excel data*

# Reading Data from a Database

Data from database sources are easily imported using the Database Wizard. Any database that uses ODBC (Open Database Connectivity) drivers can be read directly by SPSS after the drivers are installed. ODBC drivers for many database formats are supplied on the installation CD. Additional drivers can be obtained from third-party vendors. One of the most common database applications, Microsoft Access, is discussed in this example.

▶ From the menus choose:
File
  Open Database
    New Query...

Figure 3-7
*Database Wizard Welcome dialog box*

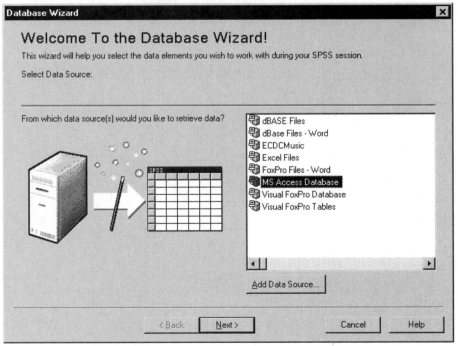

▶ Select MS Access Database from the list of data sources and click Next.

If MS Access Database is not listed here, you need to run *Microsoft Data Access Pack.exe*, which can be found in the Microsoft Data Access Pack folder on the CD.

Figure 3-8
*ODBC Driver Login dialog box*

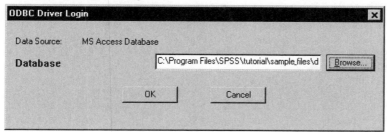

▶ Click Browse to navigate to the Access database file that you want to open.

Figure 3-9
*Open File dialog box*

▶ Select *demo.mdb* and click Open to continue.

▶ Click OK in the login dialog box.

In the next step, you can specify the tables and variables that you want to import.

Figure 3-10
*Select Data step*

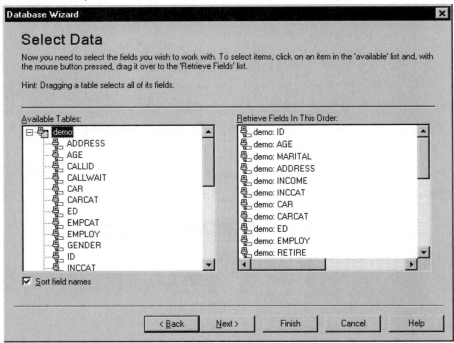

▶ Drag the entire demo table to the Retrieve Fields in This Order list.

▶ Click Next.

In the next step, you select which records (cases) to import.

**Figure 3-11**
*Limit Retrieved Cases step*

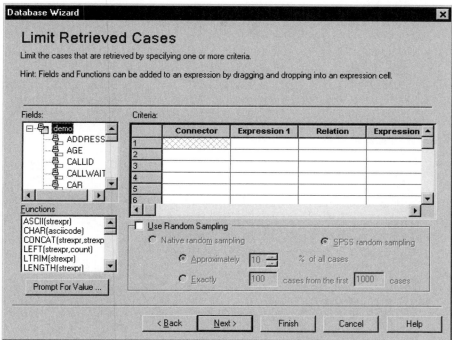

If you do not want to import all cases, you can import a subset of cases (for example, males older than 30), or you can import a random sample of cases from the data source. For large data sources, you may want to limit the number of cases to a small, representative sample to reduce the processing time.

▶ Click Next to continue.

If you are in distributed mode, connected to a remote server (available with SPSS Server), the next step allows you to aggregate the data before reading it into SPSS.

Figure 3-12
*Aggregate Data step*

You can also aggregate data after reading it into SPSS, but pre-aggregating may save time for large data sources.

▶ For this example, you don't need to aggregate the data. If you see this step in the Database Wizard, click Next.

Field names are used to create variable names. If necessary, the names are converted to valid variable names. The original field names are preserved as variable labels. You can also change the variable names before importing the database.

Figure 3-13
*Define Variables step*

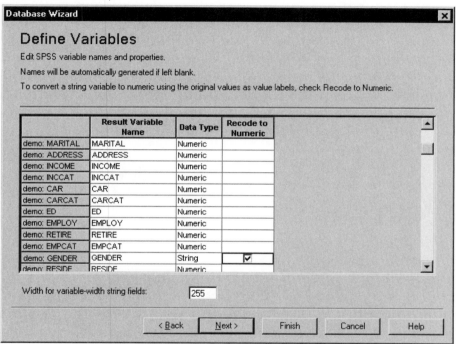

▶ Click the Recode to Numeric cell in the Gender field. This option converts string variables to integer variables and retains the original value as the value label for the new variable.

▶ Click Next to continue.

If you are in distributed mode, connected to a remote server (available with SPSS Server), the next step allows you sort the data before reading it into SPSS.

You can also sort data after reading it into SPSS, but presorting may save time for large data sources.

▶ For this example, you don't need to sort the data. If you see this step in the Database Wizard, click Next.

The SQL statement created from your selections in the Database Wizard appears in the Results step. This statement can be executed now or saved to a file for later use.

Figure 3-14
*Results step*

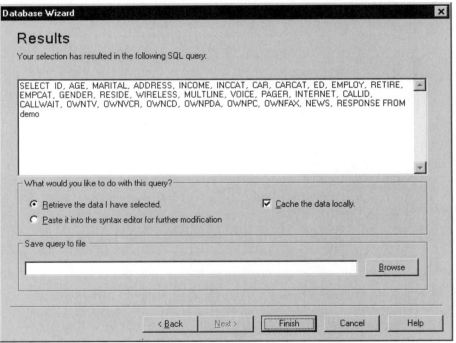

▶ Click Finish to import the data.

All of the data in the Access database that you selected to import are now available in the SPSS Data Editor.

Figure 3-15
*Data imported from an Access database*

# Reading Data from a Text File

Text files are another common source of data. Many spreadsheet programs and databases can save their contents in one of many text file formats. Comma or tab-delimited files refer to rows of data that use commas or tabs to indicate each variable. In this example, the data are tab delimited.

*Chapter 3*

▶ From the menus choose:

File
  Read Text Data...

▶ Choose Text (*.txt) from the Files of Type list.

Figure 3-16
*Open File dialog box*

▶ Select *demo.txt* and click Open to read the selected file.

The Text Import Wizard guides you through the process of defining how the specified text file should be interpreted.

**Figure 3-17**
*Text Import Wizard - Step 1 of 6*

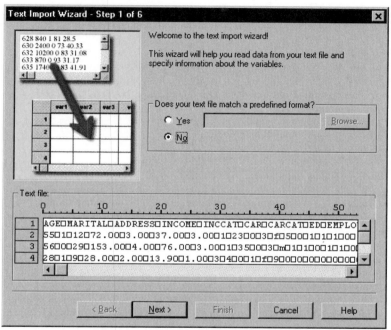

▶ In Step 1, you can choose a predefined format or create a new format in the wizard. Select No to indicate that a new format should be created.

▶ Click Next to continue.

As stated earlier, this file uses tab-delimited formatting. Also, the variable names are defined on the top line of this file.

**Figure 3-18**
*Text Import Wizard - Step 2 of 6*

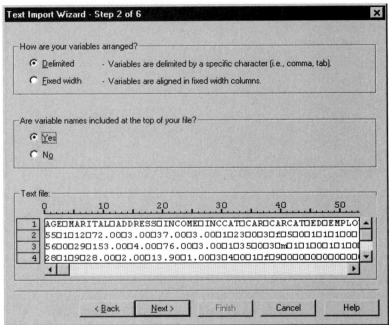

▶ Select Delimited to indicate that the data use a delimited formatting structure.

▶ Select Yes to indicate that variable names should be read from the top of the file.

▶ Click Next to continue.

▶ Type 2 in the top section of next dialog box to indicate that the first row of data starts on the second line of the text file.

**Figure 3-19**
*Text Import Wizard - Step 3 of 6*

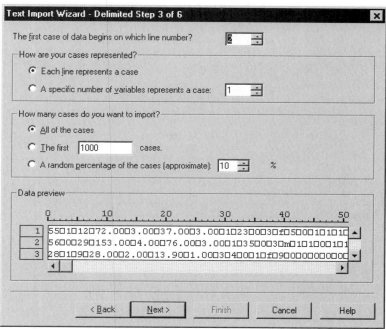

▶ Keep the default values for the remainder of this dialog box, and click Next to continue.

The Data preview in Step 4 provides you with a quick way to ensure that your data are being properly read by SPSS.

**Figure 3-20**
*Text Import Wizard - Step 4 of 6*

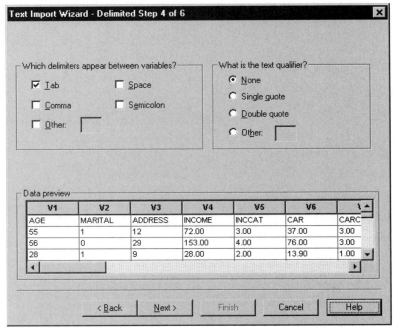

▶ Select Tab and deselect the other options.

▶ Click Next to continue.

Because the variable names may have been truncated to fit SPSS formatting requirements, this dialog box gives you the opportunity to edit any undesirable names.

**Figure 3-21**
*Text Import Wizard - Step 5 of 6*

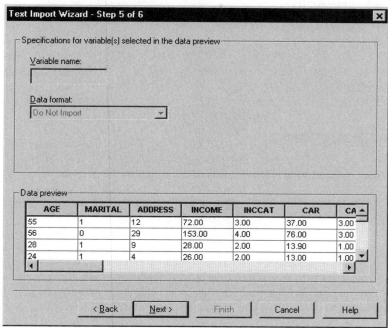

Data types can be defined here as well. For example, it's safe to assume that the income variable is meant to contain a certain dollar amount.

To change a data type:

▶ Under Data preview, select the variable you want to change, which is *Income* in this case.

▶ Select Dollar from the Data format drop-down list.

**Figure 3-22**
*Change the data type*

▶ Click Next to continue.

Figure 3-23
*Text Import Wizard - Step 6 of 6*

▶ Leave the default selections in this dialog box, and click Finish to import the data.

## Saving Data

To save an SPSS data file, the Data Editor window must be the active window.

▶ From the menus choose:
File
 Save

▶ Browse to the desired directory.

▶ Type a name for the file in the File name text box.

The Variables button can be used to select which variables in the Data Editor are saved to the SPSS data file. By default, all variables in the Data Editor are retained.

▶ Click Save.

The name in the title bar of the Data Editor will change to the filename you specified. This confirms that the file has been successfully saved as an SPSS data file. The file contains both variable information (names, type, and, if provided, labels and missing value codes), and all data values.

# *Using the Data Editor*

The Data Editor displays the contents of the active data file. The information in the Data Editor consists of variables and cases.

- In Data View, columns represent variables and rows represent cases (observations).

- In Variable View, each row is a variable, and each column is an attribute associated with that variable.

Variables are used to represent the different types of data that you have compiled. A common analogy is that of a survey. The response to each question on a survey is equivalent to a variable. Variables come in many different types, including numbers, strings, currency, and dates.

## *Entering Numeric Data*

Data can be entered into the Data Editor, which may be useful for small data files or for making minor edits to larger data files.

▶ Click the Variable View tab at the bottom of the Data Editor window.

Define the variables that are going to be used. In this case, only three variables are needed: *age*, *marital status*, and *income*.

Figure 4-1
*Variable names in Variable View*

▶ In the first row of the first column, type age.

▶ In the second row, type marital.

▶ In the third row, type income.

New variables are automatically given a numeric data type.

If you don't enter variable names, unique names are automatically created. However, these names are not descriptive and are not recommended for large data files.

▶ Click the Data View tab to continue entering the data.

The names that you entered in Variable View are now the headings for the first three columns in Data View.

Begin entering data in the first row, starting at the first column.

Figure 4-2
*Values entered in Data View*

▶ In the *age* column, type 55.

▶ In the *marital* column, type 1.

▶ In the *income* column, type 72000.

▶ Move the cursor to the first column of the second row to add the next subject's data.

▶ In the *age* column, type 53.

▶ In the *marital* column, type 0.

▶ In the *income* column, type 153000.

Currently, the *age* and *marital* columns display decimal points, even though their values are intended to be integers. To hide the decimal points in these variables:

▶ Click the Variable View tab at the bottom of the Data Editor window.

▶ Select the *Decimals* column in the *age* row and type 0 to hide the decimal.

▶ Select the *Decimals* column in the *marital* row and type 0 to hide the decimal.

**Figure 4-3**
*Updated decimal property for age and marital*

# Entering String Data

Non-numeric data, such as strings of text, can also be entered into the Data Editor.

▶ Click the Variable View tab at the bottom of the Data Editor window.

▶ In the first cell of the first empty row, type **sex** for the variable name.

▶ Click the *Type* cell.

▶ Click the button in the *Type* cell to open the Variable Type dialog box.

**Figure 4-4**
*Button shown in Type cell for sex*

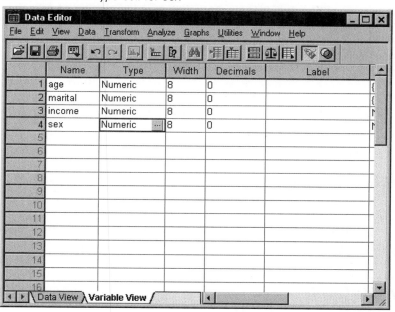

▶ Select String to specify the variable type.

▶ Click OK to save your changes and return to the Data Editor.

Figure 4-5
*Variable Type dialog box*

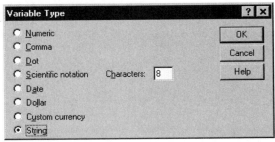

# Defining Data

In addition to defining data types, you can also define descriptive variable and value labels for variable names and data values. These descriptive labels are used in statistical reports and charts.

## Adding a Variable Label

Labels are meant to provide descriptions of variables. These descriptions are often longer versions of variable names. Labels can be up to 256 characters long. These labels are used in your output to identify the different variables.

▶ Click the Variable View tab at the bottom of the Data Editor window.

▶ In the *Label* column of the *age* row, type Respondent's Age.

▶ In the *Label* column of the *marital* row, type Marital Status.

▶ In the *Label* column of the *income* row, type Household Income.

▶ In the *Label* column of the *sex* row, type Gender.

Figure 4-6
*Variable labels entered in Variable View*

| | Name | Type | Width | Decimals | Label | |
|---|---|---|---|---|---|---|
| 1 | age | Numeric | 8 | 0 | Respondent's Age | |
| 2 | marital | Numeric | 8 | 0 | Marital Status | |
| 3 | income | Numeric | 8 | 2 | Household Income | |
| 4 | sex | String | 8 | 0 | Gender | |

## Changing Variable Type and Format

The *Type* column displays the current data type for each variable. The most common are numeric and string, but many other formats are supported. In the current data file, the *income* variable is defined as a numeric type.

▶ Click the *Type* cell for the *income* row, and then click the button to open the Variable Type dialog box.

▶ Select Dollar in the Variable Type dialog box.

**Figure 4-7**
*Variable Type dialog box*

The formatting options for the currently selected data type are displayed.

▶ Select the format of this currency. For this example, select $###,###,###.

▶ Click OK to save your changes.

## Adding Value Labels for Numeric Variables

Value labels provide a method for mapping your variable values to a string label. In the case of this example, there are two acceptable values for the *marital* variable. A value of 0 means that the subject is single, and a value of 1 means that he or she is married.

▶ Click the *Values* cell for the *marital* row, and then click the button to open the Value Labels dialog box.

The **value** is the actual numeric value.

The **value label** is the string label applied to the specified numeric value.

▶ Type 0 in the Value field.

▶ Type Single in the Value Label field.

▶ Click Add to add this label to the list.

Figure 4-8
*Value Labels dialog box*

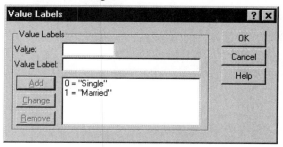

▶ Repeat the process, this time typing 1 in the Value field and **Married** in the Value Label field.

▶ Click Add, and then click OK to save your changes and return to the Data Editor.

These labels can also be displayed in Data View, which can help to make your data more readable.

▶ Click the Data View tab at the bottom of the Data Editor window.

▶ From the menus choose:
View
  Value Labels

The labels are now displayed in a list when you enter values in the Data Editor. This has the benefit of suggesting a valid response and providing a more descriptive answer.

Figure 4-9

*Value labels displayed in Data View*

## Adding Value Labels for String Variables

String variables may require value labels as well. For example, your data may use single letters, *M* or *F*, to identify the sex of the subject. Value labels can be used to specify that *M* stands for *Male* and *F* stands for *Female*.

▶ Click the Variable View tab at the bottom of the Data Editor window.

▶ Click the *Values* cell in the *sex* row, and then click the button to open the Value Labels dialog box.

▶ Type F in the Value field, and then type Female in the Value Label field.

▶ Click Add to add this label to your data file.

**Figure 4-10**
*Value Labels dialog box*

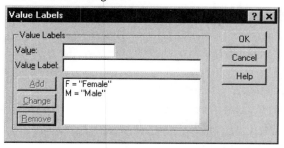

▶ Repeat the process, this time typing M in the Value field and Male in the Value Label field.

▶ Click Add, and then click OK to save your changes and return to the Data Editor.

Because string values are case sensitive, you should make sure that you are consistent. A lowercase *m* is not the same as an uppercase *M*.

## Using Value Labels for Data Entry

In a previous example, we chose to have value labels displayed rather than the actual data by selecting Value Labels from the View menu. You can use these values for data entry.

▶ Click the Data View tab at the bottom of the Data Editor window.

▶ In the first row, select the cell for *sex* and select Male from the drop-down list.

▶ In the second row, select the cell for *sex* and select Female from the drop-down list.

**Figure 4-11**
*Using variable labels to select values*

Only defined values are listed, which helps to ensure that the data entered are in a format that you expect.

## Handling Missing Data

Missing or invalid data are generally too common to ignore. Survey respondents may refuse to answer certain questions, may not know the answer, or may answer in an unexpected format. If you don't take steps to filter or identify these data, your analysis may not provide accurate results.

For numeric data, empty data fields or fields containing invalid entries are handled by converting the fields to system missing, which is identifiable by a single period.

Figure 4-12
*Missing values displayed as periods*

The reason a value is missing may be important to your analysis. For example, you may find it useful to distinguish between those who refused to answer a question and those who didn't answer a question because it was not applicable.

## Missing Values for a Numeric Variable

▶ Click the Variable View tab at the bottom of the Data Editor window.

▶ Click the *Missing* cell in the *age* row, and then click the button to open the Missing Values dialog box.

In this dialog box, you can specify up to three distinct missing values, or a range of values plus one additional discrete value.

**Figure 4-13**
*Missing Values dialog box*

▶ Select Discrete missing values.

▶ Type 999 in the first text box and leave the other two empty.

▶ Click OK to save your changes and return to the Data Editor.

Now that the missing data value has been added, a label can be applied to that value.

▶ Click the *Values* cell in the *age* row, and then click the button to open the Value Labels dialog box.

▶ Type 999 in the Value field.

▶ Type No Response in the Value Label field.

**Figure 4-14**
*Value Labels dialog box*

▶ Click Add to add this label to your data file.

▶ Click OK to save your changes and return to the Data Editor.

## *Missing Values for a String Variable*

Missing values for string variables are handled similarly to those for numeric values. Unlike numeric values, empty fields in string variables are not designated as system missing. Rather, they are interpreted as an empty string.

▶ Click the Variable View tab at the bottom of the Data Editor window.

▶ Click the *Missing* cell in the *sex* row, and then click the button to open the Missing Values dialog box.

▶ Select Discrete missing values.

▶ Type NR in the first text box.

Missing values for string variables are case sensitive. So, a value of *nr* is not treated as a missing value.

▶ Click OK to save your changes and return to the Data Editor.

Now you can add a label for the missing value.

▶ Click the *Values* cell in the *sex* row, and then click the button to open the Value Labels dialog box.

▶ Type NR in the Value field.

▶ Type No Response in the Value Label field.

Figure 4-15
*Value Labels dialog box*

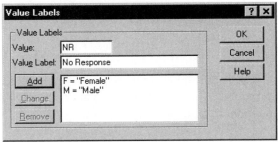

▶ Click Add to add this label to your project.

▶ Click OK to save your changes and return to the Data Editor.

## Copying and Pasting Value Attributes

Once you've defined variable attributes for a variable, you can copy these attributes and apply them to other variables.

▶ In Variable View, type agewed in the first cell of the first empty row.

Figure 4-16
*agewed variable in Variable View*

| | Name | Type | Width | Decimals | Label | |
|---|---|---|---|---|---|---|
| 1 | age | Numeric | 8 | 0 | Respondent's Age | { |
| 2 | marital | Numeric | 8 | 0 | Marital Status | { |
| 3 | income | Dollar | 12 | 0 | Household Income | ľ |
| 4 | sex | String | 8 | 0 | Gender | { |
| 5 | agewed | Numeric | 8 | 2 | Age Married | ľ |
| 6 | | | | | | |
| 7 | | | | | | |
| 8 | | | | | | |
| 9 | | | | | | |
| 10 | | | | | | |
| 11 | | | | | | |
| 12 | | | | | | |
| 13 | | | | | | |
| 14 | | | | | | |
| 15 | | | | | | |
| 16 | | | | | | |

▶ In the *Label* column, type Age Married.

▶ Click the *Values* cell in the *age* row.

▶ From the menus choose:
Edit
  Copy

▶ Click the *Values* cell in the *agewed* row.

▶ From the menus choose:
Edit
  Paste

The defined values from the *age* variable are now applied to the *agewed* variable.

Figure 4-17
*Values pasted for agewed*

| | Type | Width | Decimals | Label | Values | Mi |
|---|---|---|---|---|---|---|
| 1 | Numeric | 8 | 0 | Respondent's | {999, No Resp | 999 |
| 2 | Numeric | 9 | 0 | Marital Status | {0, Single}... | None |
| 3 | Dollar | 12 | 0 | Household Inc | None | None |
| 4 | String | 8 | 0 | Gender | {F, Female}... | NR |
| 5 | Numeric | 8 | 2 | Age Married | {999.00, No Re | None |
| 6 | | | | | | |
| 7 | | | | | | |
| 8 | | | | | | |
| 9 | | | | | | |
| 10 | | | | | | |
| 11 | | | | | | |
| 12 | | | | | | |
| 13 | | | | | | |
| 14 | | | | | | |
| 15 | | | | | | |
| 16 | | | | | | |

To apply the attribute to multiple variables, simply select multiple target cells (click and drag down the column).

Figure 4-18
*Multiple cells selected*

When you paste the attribute, it is applied to all of the selected cells.

**Figure 4-19**
*Values pasted into multiple cells*

| | Name | Type | Width | Decimals | Label | Value |
|---|---|---|---|---|---|---|
| 1 | age | Numeric | 8 | 0 | Respondent's | {999, No |
| 2 | marital | Numeric | 9 | 0 | Marital Status | {0, Single |
| 3 | income | Dollar | 12 | 0 | Household Inc | None |
| 4 | sex | String | 8 | 0 | Gender | {F, Fema |
| 5 | agewed | Numeric | 8 | 2 | Age Married | {999.00, |
| 6 | var00001 | Numeric | 8 | 2 | | {999.00, |
| 7 | var00002 | Numeric | 8 | 2 | | {999.00, |
| 8 | var00003 | Numeric | 8 | 2 | | {999.00, |
| 9 | | | | | | |
| 10 | | | | | | |
| 11 | | | | | | |
| 12 | | | | | | |
| 13 | | | | | | |
| 14 | | | | | | |
| 15 | | | | | | |
| 16 | | | | | | |

New variables are automatically created if you paste the values into empty rows.

You can also copy all of the attributes from one variable to another.

▶ Click the *row number* in the *marital* row.

Figure 4-20
*Selected row*

▶ From the menus choose:
Edit
  Copy

▶ Click the row number of the first empty row.

▶ From the menus choose:
Edit
  Paste

All of the attributes of the *marital* variable are applied to the new variable.

**Figure 4-21**
*Values pasted into row*

| | Name | Type | Width | Decimals | Label | Values |
|---|---|---|---|---|---|---|
| 1 | age | Numeric | 8 | 0 | Respondent's Age | {999, No Resp |
| 2 | marital | Numeric | 8 | 0 | Marital Status | {0, Single}... |
| 3 | income | Dollar | 12 | 0 | Household Income | None |
| 4 | sex | String | 8 | 0 | Gender | {F, Female}... |
| 5 | agewed | Numeric | 8 | 2 | Age Married | {999.00, No F |
| 6 | var00001 | Numeric | 8 | 2 | | {999.00, No F |
| 7 | var00002 | Numeric | 8 | 2 | | {999.00, No F |
| 8 | var00003 | Numeric | 8 | 2 | | {999.00, No F |
| 9 | var00004 | Numeric | 8 | 0 | Marital Status | {0, Single}... |
| 10 | | | | | | |
| 11 | | | | | | |
| 12 | | | | | | |
| 13 | | | | | | |
| 14 | | | | | | |
| 15 | | | | | | |
| 16 | | | | | | |

Data View ╲ Variable View ╱

## Defining Variable Properties for Categorical Variables

For categorical (nominal, ordinal) data, Define Variable Properties can help you define value labels and other variable properties. Define Variable Properties:

- Scans the actual data values and lists all unique data values for each selected variable.

- Identifies unlabeled values and provides an "auto-label" feature.

- Provides the ability to copy defined value labels from another variable to the selected variable or from the selected variable to multiple additional variables.

This example uses the data file *demo.sav*. This data file already has defined value labels; so before we start, let's enter a value for which there is no defined value label:

► In Data View of the Data Editor, click the first data cell for the variable *ownpc* (you may have to scroll to the right) and enter the value **99**.

► From the menus choose:

Data
  Define Variable Properties...

Figure 4-22
*Initial Define Variable Properties dialog box*

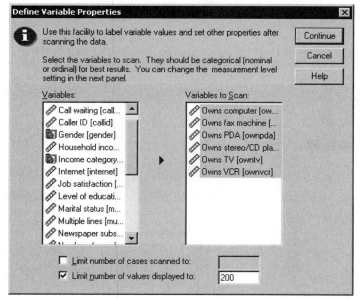

In the initial Define Variable Properties dialog box, you select the nominal or ordinal variables for which you want to define value labels and/or other properties.

Since Define Variable Properties relies on actual values in the data file to help you make good choices, it needs to read the data file first. This can take some time if your data file contains a very large number of cases, so this dialog box also allows you to limit the number of cases to read, or scan. Limiting the number of cases is not necessary for our sample data file. Even though it contains over 6,000 cases, it doesn't take very long to scan that many cases.

▶ Drag and drop *Owns computer [ownpc]* through *Owns VCR [ownvcr]* into the Variables to Scan list.

You might notice that the measurement level icons for all of the selected variables indicate that they are scale variables, not categorical variables. By default, all numeric variables are assigned the scale measurement level, even if the numeric values are actually just codes that represent categories. All of the selected variables in this example are really categorical variables that use the numeric values 0 and 1 to stand for *No* and *Yes*, respectively—and one of the variable properties that we'll change with Define Variable Properties is the measurement level.

▶ Click Continue.

Figure 4-23
*Define Variable Properties main dialog box*

▶ In the Scanned Variable List, select *ownpc.*

The current level of measurement for the selected variable is scale. You can change the measurement level by selecting one from the drop-down list or you can let Define Variable Properties suggest a measurement level.

▶ Click Suggest.

Figure 4-24
*Suggest Measurement Level dialog box*

Since the variable doesn't have very many different values and all of the scanned cases contain integer values, the proper measurement level is probably ordinal or nominal.

▶ Select Ordinal and then click Continue.

The measurement level for the selected variable is now ordinal.

The Value Labels Grid displays all of the unique data values for the selected variable, any defined value labels for these values, and the number of times (count) each value occurs in the scanned cases.

The value that we entered, 99, is displayed in the grid. The count is only 1 because we changed the value for only one case, and the *Label* column is empty because we haven't defined a value label for 99 yet. An X in the first column of the Scanned Variable List also indicates that the selected variable has at least one observed value without a defined value label.

▶ In the *Label* column for the value of 99, enter No answer.

▶ Then click (check) the box in the *Missing* column. This identifies the value 99 as **user missing**. Data values specified as user missing are flagged for special treatment and are excluded from most calculations.

Figure 4-25
*New variable properties defined for ownpc*

Before we complete the job of modifying the variable properties for *ownpc*, let's apply the same measurement level, value labels, and missing values definitions to the other variables in the list.

▶ In the Copy Properties group, click To Other Variables.

Figure 4-26
*Apply Labels and Level dialog box*

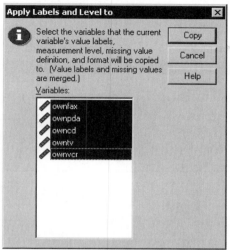

In the Apply Labels and Level dialog box, select all of the variables in the list, and then click Copy.

If you select any other variable in the list in the Define Variable Properties main dialog box now, you'll see that they are all now ordinal variables, with a value of 99 defined as user missing and a value label of *No answer*.

Figure 4-27
*New variable properties defined for ownfax*

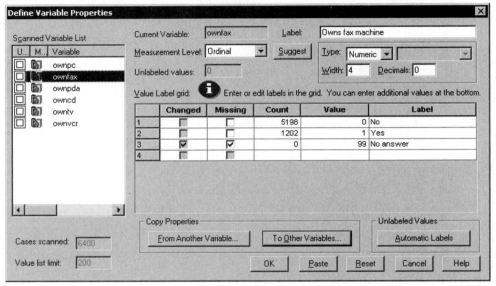

▶ Click OK to save all of the variable properties that you have defined.

# Examining Summary Statistics for Individual Variables

This chapter discusses simple summary measures and how the level of measurement of a variable influences the types of statistics that should be used. We will use the data file *demo.sav*.

## Level of Measurement

Different summary measures are appropriate for different types of data, depending on the level of measurement:

**Categorical.** Data with a limited number of distinct values or categories (for example, gender or marital status). Also referred to as qualitative data. Categorical variables can be string (alphanumeric) data or numeric variables that use numeric codes to represent categories (for example, 0 = Unmarried and 1 = Married). There are two basic types of categorical data:

- **Nominal.** Categorical data where there is no inherent order to the categories. For example, a job category of "sales" isn't higher or lower than a job category of "marketing" or "research."

- **Ordinal.** Categorical data where there is a meaningful order of categories, but there isn't a measurable distance between categories. For example, there is an order to the values high, medium, and low, but the "distance" between the values can't be calculated.

**Scale.** Data measured on an interval or ratio scale, where the data values indicate both the order of values and the distance between values. For example, a salary of $72,195 is higher than a salary of $52,398, and the distance between the two values is $19,797. Also referred to as quantitative or continuous data.

# Summary Measures for Categorical Data

For categorical data, the most typical summary measure is the number or percentage of cases in each category. The **mode** is the category with the greatest number of cases. For ordinal data, the **median** (the value above and below which half the cases fall) may also be a useful summary measure if there is a large number of categories.

The Frequencies procedure produces frequency tables that display both the number and percentage of cases for each observed value of a variable.

▶ From the menus choose:

Analyze
  Descriptive Statistics
    Frequencies...

▶ Select *Owns PDA (ownpda)* and *Owns TV (owntv)* and move them into the Variable(s) list.

Figure 5-1
*Categorical variables selected for analysis*

▶ Click OK to run the procedure.

Figure 5-2
*Frequency tables*

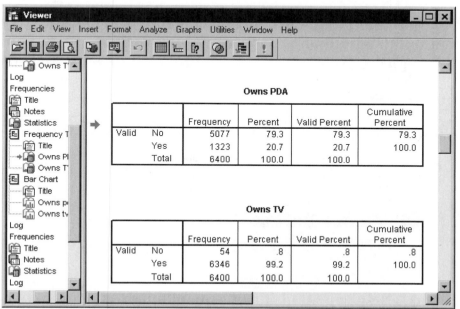

The frequency tables are displayed in the Viewer window. The frequency tables reveal that only about 21% of the people own PDAs, but almost everybody owns a TV (99.2%). This might not be an interesting revelation, although it might be interesting to find out more about the small group of people who do not own televisions.

## Charts for Categorical Data

You can graphically display the information in a frequency table with a bar chart or pie chart.

▶ Open the Frequencies dialog box again. (The two variables should still be selected.)

You can use the Dialog Recall button on the toolbar to quickly return to recently used procedures.

**Figure 5-3**
*Dialog Recall tool*

▶ Click Charts.

▶ Select Bar charts and then click Continue.

**Figure 5-4**
*Frequencies Charts dialog box*

▶ Click OK in the main dialog box to run the procedure.

Figure 5-5
*Bar chart*

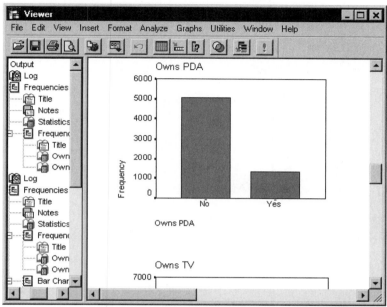

In addition to the frequency tables, the same information is now displayed in the form of bar charts, making it easy to see that most people do not own PDAs but almost everyone owns a TV.

## Summary Measures for Scale Variables

There are many summary measures available for scale variables, including:

- **Measures of central tendency.** The most common measures of central tendency are the **mean** (arithmetic average) and **median** (value above and below which half the cases fall).

- **Measures of dispersion.** Statistics that measure the amount of variation or spread in the data include the standard deviation, minimum, and maximum.

▶ Open the Frequencies dialog box again.

▶ Click Reset to clear any previous settings.

▶ Select *Household income in thousands (income)* and move it into the Variable(s) list.

**Figure 5-6**
*Scale variable selected for analysis*

▶ Click Statistics.

▶ Select Mean, Median, Std. deviation, Minimum, and Maximum.

**Figure 5-7**
*Frequencies Statistics dialog box*

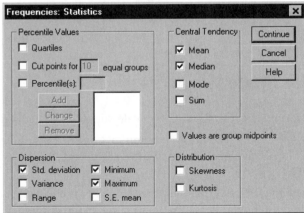

▶ Click Continue.

▶ Deselect Display frequency tables in the main dialog box. (Frequency tables are usually not useful for scale variables since there may be almost as many distinct values as there are cases in the data file.)

▶ Click OK to run the procedure.

The Frequencies Statistics table is displayed in the Viewer window.

Figure 5-8
*Frequencies Statistics table*

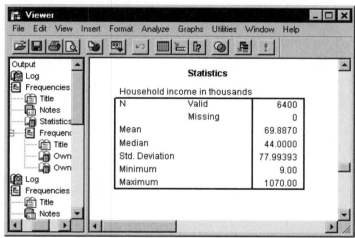

In this example, there is a large difference between the mean and the median, with the mean being more than 25,000 greater than the median. This indicates that the values are not normally distributed. We can visually check the distribution with a histogram.

## *Histograms for Scale Variables*

▶ Open the Frequencies dialog box again.

▶ Click Charts.

▶ Select Histograms and With normal curve.

Figure 5-9
*Frequencies Charts dialog box*

▶ Click Continue and click OK in the main dialog box to run the procedure.

**Figure 5-10**
*Histogram*

The majority of cases are clustered at the lower end of the scale, with most falling below 100,000. There are, however, a few cases in the 500,000 range and beyond (too few to even be visible without modifying the histogram). These high values for only a few cases have a significant effect on the mean but little or no effect on the median, making the median a better indicator of central tendency in this example.

# *Working with Output*

The results from running a statistical procedure are displayed in the Viewer. The output produced can be statistical tables, charts or graphs, or text, depending on the choices you make when you run the procedure. This chapter uses the files *viewertut.spo* and *demo.sav*.

## *Using the Viewer*

Figure 6-1
*SPSS Viewer*

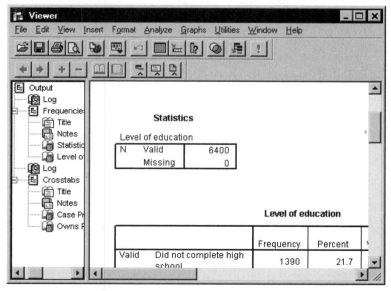

The Viewer window is divided into two panes. The **outline pane** contains an outline of all of the information stored in the Viewer. The **contents pane** contains statistical tables, charts, and text output.

Use the scrollbars to navigate through the window's contents, both vertically and horizontally. For easier navigation, click an item in the outline pane to display it in the contents pane.

If you find that there isn't enough room in the Viewer to see an entire table or that the outline view is too narrow, you can easily resize the window.

▶ Click and drag the right border of the outline pane to change its width.

An open book icon in the outline pane indicates that it is currently visible in the Viewer, although it may not currently be in the visible portion of the contents pane.

▶ To hide a table or chart, double-click its book icon in the outline pane.

The open book icon changes to a closed book icon, signifying that the information associated with it is now hidden.

▶ To redisplay the hidden output, double-click the closed book icon.

You can also hide all of the output from a particular statistical procedure or all of the output in the Viewer.

▶ Click the box with the minus sign (−) to the left of the procedure whose results you want to hide, or click the box next to the topmost item in the outline pane to hide all of the output.

Figure 6-2
*Hidden output in the Viewer*

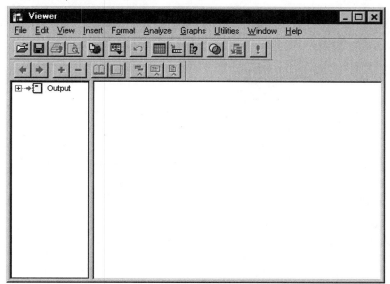

The outline collapses, visually indicating that these results are hidden.

You can also change the order in which the output is displayed.

▶ In the outline pane, click on the items you want to move.

▶ Drag the selected items to a new location in the outline and release the mouse button.

Figure 6-3
*Reordered output in the Viewer*

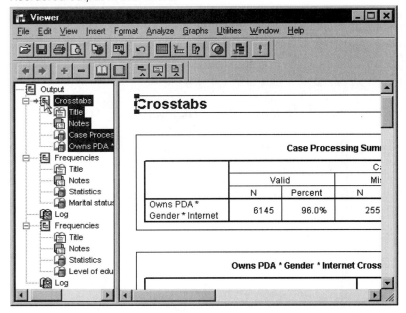

You can also move output items by clicking and dragging them in the contents pane.

# Using the Pivot Table Editor

The results from most statistical procedures are displayed in **pivot tables**.

## Accessing Output Definitions

Many statistical terms are displayed in the output. Definitions of these terms can be accessed directly in the Viewer.

▶ Double-click the *Owns PDA * Gender * Internet Crosstabulation* table.

▶ Right-click *Expected Count* and select What's This? from the pop-up context menu.

The definition is displayed in a pop-up window.

Figure 6-4
*Pop-up definition*

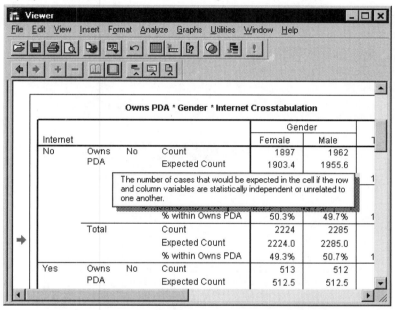

## Pivoting Tables

The default tables produced may not display information as neatly or as clearly as you would like. With pivot tables, you can transpose rows and columns ("flip" the table), adjust the order of data in a table, and modify the table in many other ways. For example, you can change a short, wide table into a long, thin one by transposing rows and columns. Changing the layout of the table does not affect the results. Instead, it's a way to display your information in a different or more desirable manner.

▶ Double-click the *Owns PDA * Gender * Internet Crosstabulation* table.

▶ If the Pivoting Trays window is not visible, from the menus choose:

Pivot
  Pivoting Trays

Pivoting Trays provide a way to move data between columns, rows, and layers.

**Figure 6-5**
*Pivoting Trays*

▶ Click one of the pivot icons to see what it represents. The shaded area in the table indicates what will be moved when you move the pivot icon. A pop-up label also indicates what the icon represents in the table.

**Figure 6-6**
*Pivot icon labels*

▶ Drag the Statistics pivot icon from the Row dimension to the bottom of the Column dimension. The table is immediately reconfigured to reflect your changes.

The order of the pivot icons in a dimension reflects the order of the elements in the table.

**Figure 6-7**
*Pivoting tray icon associations*

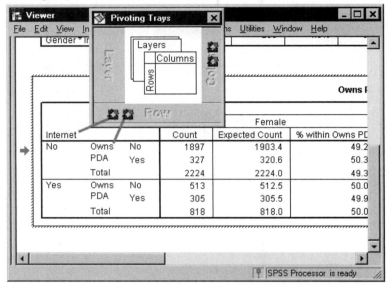

▶ Drag the *Owns PDA* icon to the left of the *Internet* icon and release the mouse button to reverse the order of these two rows

## Creating and Displaying Layers

Layers can be useful for large tables with nested categories of information. By creating layers, you simplify the look of the table, making it easier to read. Layers work best when the table has at least three variables.

▶ Double-click the *Owns PDA * Gender * Internet Crosstabulation* table.

▶ If the Pivoting Trays window is not visible, from the menus choose:
Pivot
  Pivoting Trays

▶ Drag the *Gender* pivot icon to the Layer dimension.

Figure 6-8
*Gender pivot icon in the Layer dimension*

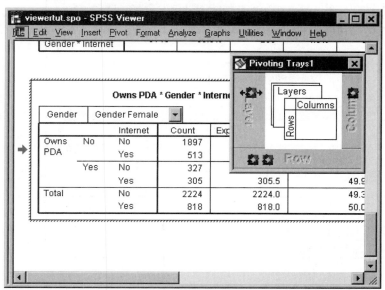

To view the different layers, you can either click the arrows on the layer pivot icon, or you can select a layer from the drop-down list in the table.

Figure 6-9
*Choosing a layer*

## Editing Tables

Unless you've taken the time to create a custom TableLook, pivot tables are created with standard formatting. You can change the formatting of any text within a table. Formats that you can change include font name, font size, font style (bold or italic), and color.

▶ Double-click the *Level of education* table.

▶ If the Formatting toolbar is not visible, from the menus choose:
  View
    Toolbar

▶ Click the title text, *Level of education*.

▶ From the drop-down list of font sizes on the toolbar, select 12.

► To change the color of the title text, click the Text Color tool and select a color.

Figure 6-10
*Reformatted title text in the pivot table*

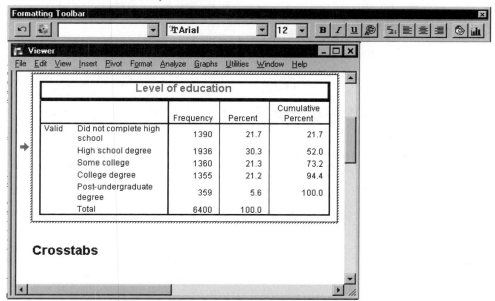

You can also edit the contents of tables and labels. For example, you can change the title of this table.

► Double-click the title.

► Type Education Level for the new label.

Note that if you change the values in a table, totals and other statistics are not recalculated.

## *Hiding Rows and Columns*

Some of the data displayed in a table may not be useful or it may unnecessarily complicate the table. Fortunately, you can hide entire rows or columns without losing any data.

▶ Double-click the *Education Level* table.

▶ Ctrl-Alt-click on the *Valid Percent* column label to select all of the cells in that column.

▶ Right-click the highlighted column and select Hide Category from the pop-up context menu.

The column is now hidden but not deleted.

To redisplay the column:

▶ From the menus choose:
View
   Show All

Rows can be hidden and displayed in the same way as columns.

## *Changing Data Display Formats*

You can easily change the display format of data in pivot tables.

▶ Double-click the *Education Level* table.

▶ Click on the *Percent* column label to select it.

▶ From the menus choose:
Edit
   Select
      Data Cells

▶ From the menus choose:

Format
  Cell Properties

▶ Type 0 in the Decimals field to hide all decimal points in this column.

Figure 6-11
*Cell Properties dialog box*

You can also change the data type and format in this dialog box.

▶ Select the type that you want from the Category list, and then select the format for that type in the Format list.

▶ Click OK to apply your changes and return to the Viewer.

Figure 6-12
*Decimals hidden in Percent column*

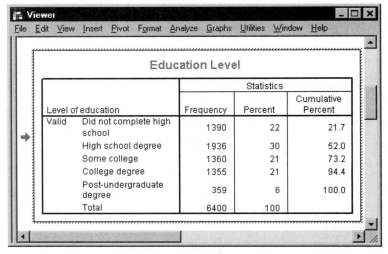

The decimals are now hidden in the *Percent* column.

# TableLooks

The look and feel of your tables are a critical part of providing clear, concise, and meaningful results. For example, if your table is difficult to read, the information contained within that table may not be easily understood.

## Using Predefined Formats

▶ Double-click the *Marital status* table.

▶ From the menus choose:
Format
  TableLooks...

The TableLooks dialog box lists a variety of predefined styles. Select a style from the list to preview it in the Sample window to the right.

Figure 6-13
*TableLooks dialog box*

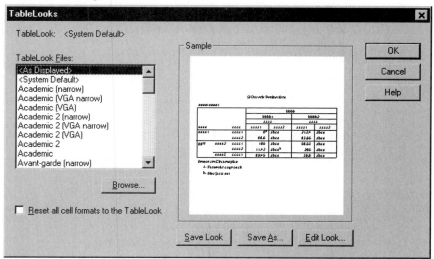

You can use a style as is, or you can edit an existing style to better suit your needs.

▶ To use an existing style, select one and click OK.

## Customizing TableLook Styles

You can customize a format to fit your specific needs. Almost all aspects of a table can be customized, from the background color to the border styles.

▶ Double-click the *Marital status* table.

▶ From the menus choose:
Format
TableLooks...

▶ Select the style that is closest to your desired format and click **Edit Look**.

▶ Click the **Cell Formats** tab to view the formatting options.

**Figure 6-14**
*Table Properties dialog box*

The formatting options include font name, font size, style, and color. Additional options include alignment, shading, foreground and background colors, and margin sizes.

The Sample window provides a preview of how the formatting changes affect your table. Each area of the table can have different formatting styles. For example, you probably wouldn't want the title to have the same style as the data. To select a table area to edit, you can either choose the area by name in the Area drop-down list, or you can click the area that you want to change in the Sample window.

▶ Select **Title** from the Area drop-down list.

▶ Select a new color from the Background drop-down list.

The Sample window shows the new style.

▶ Click OK to return to the TableLooks dialog box.

You can save your new style, which allows you to apply it to future tables easily.

▶ Click Save As.

▶ Navigate to the desired target directory and enter a name for your new style in the File Name text box.

▶ Click Save.

▶ Click OK to apply your changes and return to the Viewer.

The table now contains the custom formatting that you specified.

**Figure 6-15**
*Custom TableLook*

## *Changing the Default Table Formats*

Although you can change the format of a table after it has been created, it may be more efficient to change the default TableLook so that you do not have to change the format every time you create a table.

To change the default TableLook style for your pivot tables, from the menus choose:
Edit
    Options...

▶ Click the Pivot Tables tab in the Options dialog box.

**Figure 6-16**
*Options dialog box*

▶ Select the TableLook style that you want to use for all new tables.

Use the Sample window to see a preview of each TableLook.

▶ Click OK to save your settings and close the dialog box.

All tables that you create after changing the default TableLook automatically conform to the new formatting rules.

## *Customizing the Initial Display Settings*

The initial display settings include the alignment of objects in the Viewer, whether objects are shown or hidden by default, and the width of the Viewer window. To change these settings:

▶ From the menus choose:
Edit
  Options...

▶ Click the Viewer tab.

Figure 6-17
*Viewer options*

The settings are applied on an object-by-object basis. For example, you can customize the way charts are displayed without making any changes to the way tables are displayed. Simply select the object that you want to customize, and make the desired changes.

▶ Click the Title icon to display its settings.

▶ Click Center to display all titles in the (horizontal) center of the Viewer.

You can also hide elements, such as the log and warning messages, that tend to clutter your output. Double-clicking on an icon automatically changes that object's display property.

▶ Double-click the Warnings icon to hide warning messages in the output.

▶ Click OK to save your changes and close the dialog box.

Figure 6-18
*Centered title in the Marital status table*

Your new settings will be applied the next time you run a statistical procedure. All items that you have hidden will still be created, but they will not be visible in the contents pane. Centered items can be identified by the small symbol to the left of the item.

## *Displaying Variable and Value Labels*

In most cases, displaying the labels for variables and values is more effective than displaying the variable name or the actual data value. There may be cases, however, when you want to display both the names and the labels.

▶ From the menus choose:
Edit
  Options...

▶ Click the Output Labels tab.

Figure 6-19
*Output Labels options*

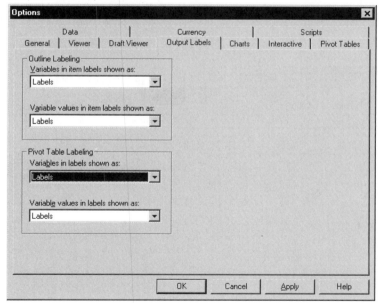

You can specify different settings for the outline and contents panes. For example, to show labels in the outline and variable names and data values in the contents:

▶ In the Pivot Table Labeling group, select Names from the Variables in Labels drop-down list to show variable names instead of labels.

▶ Then, select Values from the Variable Values in Labels drop-down list to show data values instead of labels.

Figure 6-20
*Pivot Table Labeling settings*

The new settings are applied the next time you run a statistical procedure.

Figure 6-21
*Variable names and values displayed*

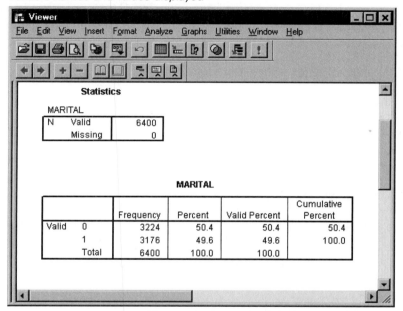

## Using Results in Other Applications

Your results can be used in many applications. For example, you may want to include a chart or graph in a presentation or report. Applications such as Microsoft's PowerPoint or Word can display your results as plain text, rich text, or as a metafile, which is a graphical representation of the output.

The following examples are specific to Microsoft Word, but they may work similarly in other word processing applications.

## *Pasting Results as Rich Text*

You can paste pivot tables into Word as native Word tables. Text formatting, such as font size and color, is not retained, but columns and rows are properly aligned. Because the table is in a text format, the data can be edited after you paste it into your document.

▶ Click the *Marital status* table in the Viewer.

▶ From the menus choose:
Edit
  Copy

▶ Open your word processing application.

▶ From the word processor's menus choose:
Edit
  Paste Special

▶ Select Formatted Text (RTF) in the Paste Special dialog box.

Figure 6-22
*Paste Special dialog box*

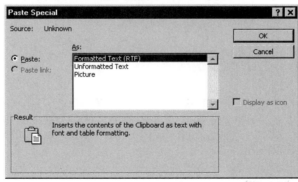

▶ Click OK to paste your results into the current document.

Figure 6-23
*Pivot table displayed in Word*

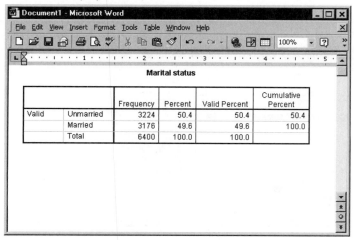

The table is now displayed in your document. You can apply custom formatting, edit the data, and resize the table to fit your needs.

## Pasting Results as Metafiles

Pasting your results as metafiles maintains the formatting of your output. Your pasted output becomes an image in the target document.

▶ Click the *Marital status* table in the Viewer.

▶ From the menus choose:
Edit
  Copy

▶ Open your word processing application.

▶ From the word processor's menus choose:
Edit
  Paste Special

▶ Select Picture in the Paste Special dialog box. (In some applications, the choice may be "metafile" instead of "Picture.")

Figure 6-24
*Paste Special dialog box*

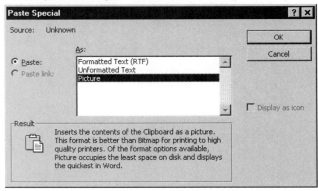

▶ Click OK to paste your results into the current document.

Figure 6-25
*Metafile displayed in Word*

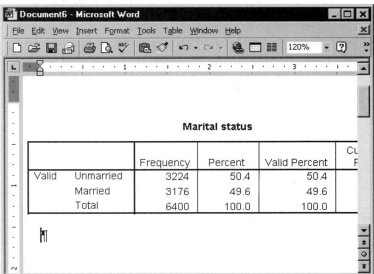

The metafile is now embedded in your document. This image is a snapshot of the *Marital status* table. Only the visible portions of the table are copied. Information in hidden categories or layers is not included in the metafile.

## Pasting Results as Text

Pivot tables can be copied to other applications as plain text. Formatting styles are not retained in this method, but you gain the ability to edit the table data after you paste it into the target application.

▶ Click the *Marital status* table in the Viewer.

▶ From the menus choose:
Edit
  Copy

▶ Open your word processing application.

▶ From the word processor's menus choose:
Edit
  Paste Special

▶ Select Unformatted Text in the Paste Special dialog box.

Figure 6-26
*Paste Special dialog box*

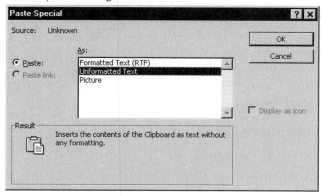

▶ Click OK to paste your results into the current document.

Figure 6-27
*Pivot table displayed in Word*

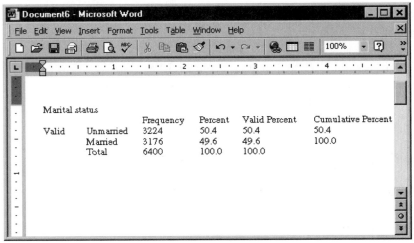

Each column of the table is separated by tabs. You can change the column widths by adjusting the tab stops in your word processing application.

## Exporting Results to Microsoft Word, PowerPoint, and Excel Files

SPSS allows you to export results to a single Microsoft Word, PowerPoint, or Excel file. You can export selected items or all items in the Viewer. If exporting to Word or PowerPoint, you can export charts. This topic uses the files *msouttut.spo* and *demo.sav*.

In the Viewer's outline pane, you can select specific items that you want to export. You do not have to select specific items.

▶ From the Viewer menus choose:
File
  Export...

There are several options for exporting the results.

**Figure 6-28**
*Export Output dialog box*

First, you can select which type of output file you want to create. For Word and PowerPoint, you can create a file that contains charts (Output Document) or one that does not contain charts (Output Document (No Charts)). Charts are embedded in Word documents as Windows metafiles. For Excel, you can create only documents that do not contain charts (Output Document (No Charts)).

► Select Output Document from the Export drop-down list.

You can save the exported Word, PowerPoint, or Excel file to any location and assign it any name that Windows allows. The default file name is *OUTPUT*, and the default path is the installation location or, if you opened or saved an output file, the location of that file. You can change the default by typing a new path or clicking Browse to locate a destination. You do not have to specify a file extension. The export functionality adds the appropriate extension.

Note the default file path in the File Name text box. You will need to know where the file is to open it.

Instead of exporting all objects in the Viewer, you can choose to export only visible objects (open books in the outline pane) or those that you selected in the outline pane. If you did not select any items in the outline pane, you do not have the option to export selected objects.

▶ Select All Objects in the Export What group.

Finally, you select the file format.

▶ Select Word/RTF file (*.doc) from the File Type drop-down list.

▶ Click OK to generate the Word file.

When you open the resulting file in Word, you can see how the results are exported. Notes, which are not visible objects, appear in Word because you chose to export all objects.

Figure 6-29
*Output.doc in Word*

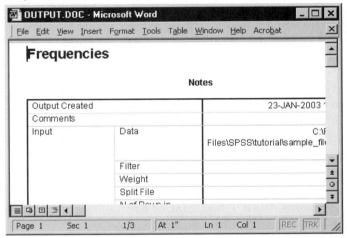

Pivot tables become Word tables, with all of the formatting of the original pivot table, including fonts, colors, borders, and so on.

Figure 6-30
*Pivot tables in Word*

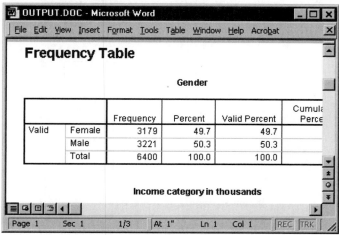

Charts become embedded Windows metafiles.

Figure 6-31
*Charts in Word*

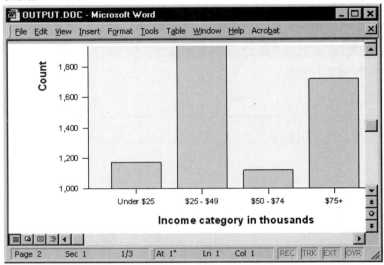

Text output is displayed in a fixed-pitch font.

Figure 6-32
*Text output in Word*

```
Income
category       Age in    Level of
in             years     education
thousands      Mean          Mean
_____

Under $25        38             2

$25 - $49        39             3

$50 - $74        43             3

$75+             49             3
```

If you export to a PowerPoint file, each exported item is placed on a separate slide. Pivot tables exported to PowerPoint become Word tables, with all of the formatting of the original pivot table, including fonts, colors, borders, and so on.

Figure 6-33
*Pivot tables in PowerPoint*

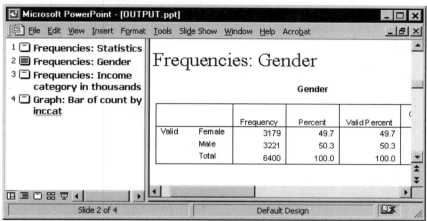

Charts selected for export to PowerPoint are embedded in the PowerPoint file.

Figure 6-34
*Charts in PowerPoint*

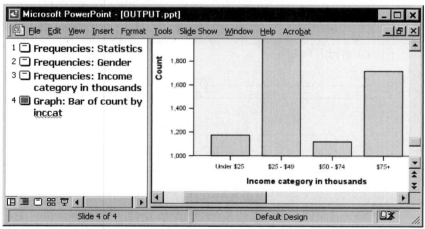

If you export to an Excel file, results are exported differently.

Figure 6-35
*Output.xls in Excel*

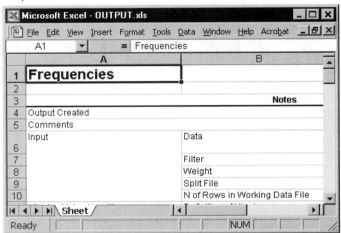

Pivot table rows, columns, and cells become Excel rows, columns, and cells.

Figure 6-36
*Pivot tables in Excel*

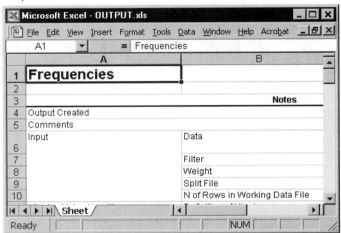

Each line in the text output is a row in the Excel file, with the entire contents of the line contained in a single cell. Charts are not exported at all.

Figure 6-37
*Text output in Excel*

## Exporting Results to HTML and Text Formats

You can also export results to HTML (hypertext markup language) and text formats and a number of graphic formats. When saving as HTML and text, all non-graphic output from SPSS can be exported into a single file and read by other programs. HTML format is commonly used for intranet and Internet Web pages, while text can be read by all word processors. In this way, SPSS output can be easily incorporated into documents on computers that do not run SPSS or onto Web pages.

When you export HTML and text output, charts can be exported as well, but not to a single file.

**Figure 6-38**
*Chart in HTML*

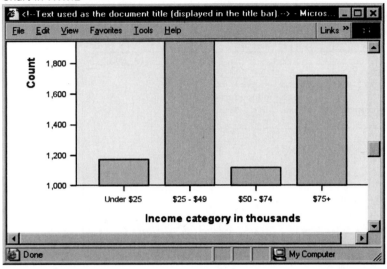

Each chart will be saved as a file in a format that you specify, and references to these graphics files will be placed in the HTML or text document created by SPSS. There is also an option to export all charts, or selected charts, in separate graphics files.

Figure 6-39
*References to graphics in HTML output*

# Creating and Editing Charts

You can create and edit a wide variety of chart types in SPSS. In these examples, we will create and edit three commonly used types of charts:

- Simple bar chart
- Pie chart
- Scatterplot with groups

## Chart Creation Basics

To demonstrate the basics of chart creation, we will create a bar chart of mean income for different levels of job satisfaction. This example uses the data file *demo.sav*.

▶ From the menus choose:
Graphs
  Bar...

In the Bar Charts dialog box, you specify what type of bar chart you want to create and what data to use in the chart.

In this example, we will create a simple chart using groups of cases. The resulting chart will show a bar for each group (category) in a single categorical variable.

Bars can also be based on summaries of separate variables (so that each variable is a bar) or values from individual cases in the data file (so that each case is a bar). You can also create a clustered or stacked bar chart. With these charts, there are multiple categorical variables.

▶ Click Simple.

▶ Click Summaries for groups of cases.

Figure 7-1
*Bar Charts dialog box*

▶ Click Define.

In the Define Simple Bar dialog box, specify the variable or variables to use for creating the chart. You want to create a chart that shows bars for the mean income of each job satisfaction category.

▶ Select *Job satisfaction* as the category axis variable.

▶ In the Bars Represent group, select Other statistic (e.g., mean).

▶ Select *Household income in thousands* as the variable to represent the bars. By default, the summary function is the mean of this variable. If you want to select a different summary function, click Change Statistic.

Figure 7-2
*Define Simple Bar dialog box*

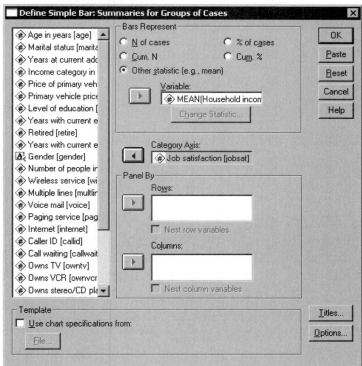

▶ Click **OK** to create the bar chart.

Figure 7-3
*Bar chart*

The bar chart reveals that respondents who are more satisfied with their jobs also tend to have higher household incomes.

# Chart Editing Basics

You can edit charts in a variety of ways. For the sample bar chart that you created, you will:

- Change colors.
- Format numbers in tick labels.
- Edit text.
- Display data value labels.
- Use chart templates.

To edit the chart, open it in the Chart Editor.

▶ Double-click the bar chart to open it in the Chart Editor.

**Figure 7-4**
*Bar chart in the Chart Editor*

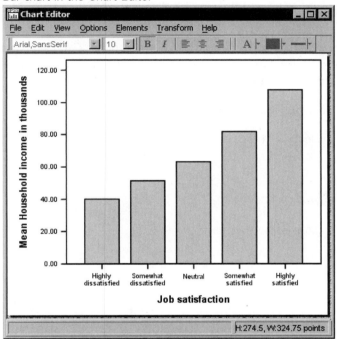

## *Selecting Chart Elements*

To edit a chart element, you first select it.

▶ Click on any one of the bars. The blue rectangles around the bars indicate that they are selected.

There are general rules for selecting elements in simple charts:

■   When no data elements are selected, click any data element to select all data elements.

■   When all data elements are selected, click a data element to select only that data element. You can select a different data element by clicking it. To select multiple data elements, click each element while pressing the Ctrl key.

*Note*: The behavior is slightly different for grouped charts. Grouped charts are discussed in the scatterplot example. For more information, see "Selecting Elements in Grouped Charts" on p. 164.

▶   To deselect all elements, press the Esc key.

▶   Click any bar to select all of the bars again.

## Using the Properties Window

▶   From the Chart Editor menus choose:
   Edit
    Properties

This opens the Properties window, showing the tabs that apply to the bars you selected. These tabs change depending on what chart element you select in the Chart Editor. For example, if you had selected a text frame instead of bars, different tabs would appear. You will use these tabs to do most chart editing.

Figure 7-5
*Properties window*

## Changing Bar Colors

First, you will change the color of the bars. You specify color attributes of data elements (excluding lines and markers) on the Fill & Border tab.

*Chapter 7*

▶ Click the Fill & Border tab.

▶ Click the swatch next to Fill to indicate that you want to change the fill color of the bars. The numbers below the swatch specify the red, green, and blue settings for the current color.

▶ Click the dark blue color, which is second from the left in the second row.

Figure 7-6
*Fill & Border tab*

▶ Click Apply.

The bars in the chart are now dark blue.

**Figure 7-7**
*Edited bar chart showing blue bars*

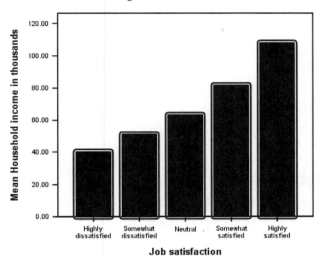

## *Formatting Numbers in Tick Labels*

Notice that the numbers on the *y* axis are scaled in thousands. The numbers also include two unnecessary decimal places. To make the chart more attractive and easier to interpret, we will change the number format in the tick labels and then edit the axis title appropriately.

▶ Select the *y* axis tick labels by clicking any one of them.

▶ To reopen the Properties window (if you closed it previously), from the menus choose:
Edit
　Properties

*Note*: From here on, we assume that the Properties window is open. If you have closed the Properties window, follow the previous step to reopen it. You can also use the keyboard shortcut Ctrl+T to reopen the window.

▶ Click the Number Format tab.

▶ You do not want the tick labels to display decimal places, so type 0 in the Decimal Places text box.

▶ Type 0.001 in the Scaling Factor text box. The scaling factor is the number by which the Chart Editor divides the displayed number. Because 0.001 is a fraction, dividing by it will *increase* the numbers in the tick labels by 1,000. Thus, the numbers will no longer be in thousands; they will be unscaled.

▶ Select Display Digit Grouping. Digit grouping uses a character (specified by your computer's locale) to mark each thousandth place in the number.

Figure 7-8
*Number Format tab*

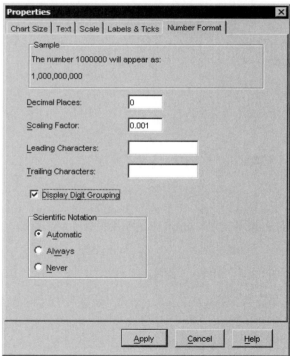

▶ Click Apply.

The tick labels reflect the new number formatting: there are no decimal places, the numbers are no longer scaled, and each thousandth place is specified with a character.

**Figure 7-9**
*Edited bar chart showing new number format*

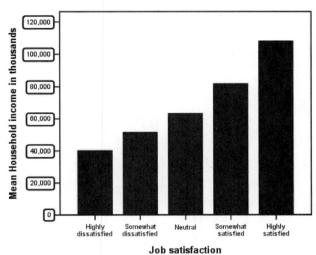

## Editing Text

Now that you have changed the number format of the tick labels, the axis title is no longer accurate. Next, you will change the axis title to reflect the new number format.

*Note*: You do not need to open the Properties window to edit text. You can edit text directly on the chart.

▶ Click the *y* axis title to select it.

▶ Click the axis title again to start edit mode. While in edit mode, the Chart Editor positions any rotated text horizontally. It also displays a flashing red bar cursor (not shown in the example).

► Delete the following text:

in thousands

► Press Enter to exit edit mode and update the axis title. The axis title now accurately describes the contents of the tick labels.

**Figure 7-10**
*Bar chart showing edited y axis title*

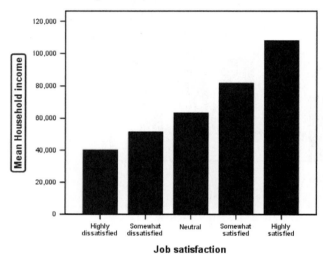

## Displaying and Editing Data Value Labels

Another common task is to show the exact values associated with the data elements (which are bars in this example). These values are displayed in data labels.

► From the Chart Editor menus choose:
Elements
  Show Data Labels

**Figure 7-11**
*Bar chart showing data value labels*

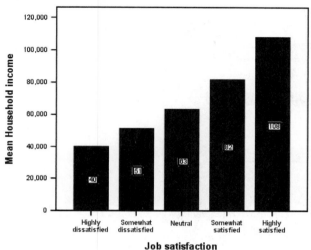

Each bar in the chart now displays the exact mean household income. Notice that the units are in thousands, so you could use the Number Format tab again to change the scaling factor. Instead, we will change the statistic shown in the data values.

▶ With the data value labels selected, click the Data Value Labels tab.

The Data Value Labels tab allows you to change various label properties. In this case, you are going to change the content of the labels so that they display the percentage of respondents in each category.

▶ Move *Household income in thousands* from the Displayed list to the Not Displayed list.

▶ Move *Percent* from the Not Displayed list to the Displayed list.

**Figure 7-12**
*Data Value Labels tab*

▶ Click Apply to update the data value labels.

As a result, the bars display the percentage of cases in each *Job satisfaction* category.

**Figure 7-13**
*Bar chart showing percentages*

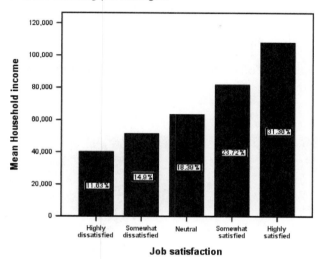

## *Using Templates*

If you make a number of routine changes to your charts, you can use a chart template to reduce the time needed to create and edit charts. A chart template saves the attributes of a specific chart. You can then apply the template when creating or editing a chart.

We will save the current chart as a template and then apply that template to create a new chart.

▶ From the menus choose:
File
  Save Chart Template...

The Save Chart Template dialog box allows you to specify which chart attributes you want to include in the template.

If you expand any of the items in the tree view, you can see which specific attributes can be saved with the chart. For example, if you expand the Scale axes portion of the tree, you can see all of the attributes of data value labels that the template will include. You can select any attribute to include it in the template.

▶ Select All settings to include all of the available chart attributes in the template.

You can also enter a description of the template. This description will be visible when applying the template.

Figure 7-14
*Save Chart Template dialog box*

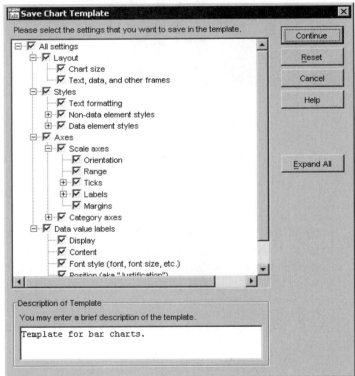

▶ Click Continue.

▶ In the Save Template dialog box, specify a location and filename for the template.

▶ When you are finished, click Save.

You can apply the template when you create a chart or in the Chart Editor. In the following example, we will apply it while creating a chart.

▶ Close the Chart Editor. The updated bar chart is shown in the Viewer.

Figure 7-15
*Updated bar chart in Viewer*

▶ From the Viewer menus choose:
Graphs
  Bar...

▶ Click Define to open the Define Simple Bar dialog box.

The dialog box "remembers" the variables that you entered when you created the original chart. However, here you will create a slightly different chart to see how applying a template formats a chart.

▶ Remove *Job satisfaction* from the Category Axis text box and replace it with *Level of education*.

▶ Select Use chart specifications from.

▶ Click File.

▶ In the Use Template from File dialog box, locate the template file that you previously saved using the Save Chart Template dialog box.

▶ Select that file and click Open.

The Define Simple Bar dialog box displays the file path of the template you selected.

**Figure 7-16**
*Define Simple Bar dialog box showing template file path*

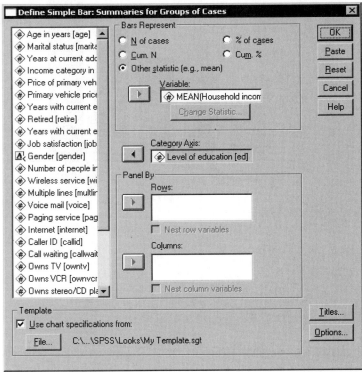

(Our example shows the path *C:\... \SPSS\Looks\My Template.sgt.*)

▶ Click OK to create the chart and apply the template.

The formatting in the new chart matches the formatting in the chart that you previously created and edited. Although the variables on the *x* axis are different, the charts otherwise resemble each other.

If you want to apply templates after you've created a chart, you can do it in the Chart Editor (choose Apply Chart Template from the File menu).

Figure 7-17
*Updated bar chart in Viewer*

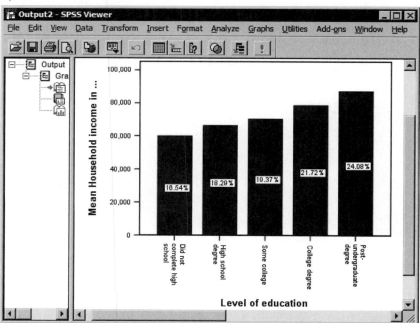

## Defining Chart Options

In addition to using templates to format charts, you can use the SPSS options to control various aspects of how charts are created.

▶ From the Data Editor or Viewer menus choose:

Edit
  Options...

The Options dialog box contains many settings for configuring SPSS. Click the Charts tab to see the available options.

Figure 7-18
*Charts tab in Options dialog box*

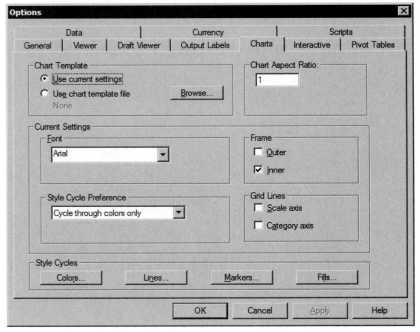

The options control how a chart is created. For each new chart, you can specify:

■ Whether to use the current settings or a template

■ The width-to-height ratio (aspect ratio)

■ If you're not using a template, the settings to use for formatting

■ The style cycles for data elements

Style cycles allow you to specify the style of data elements in new charts. In this example, we'll look at the details for the color style cycle.

▶ Click Colors to open the Data Element Colors dialog box.

For a simple chart, the Chart Editor uses one style that you specify. For grouped charts, the Chart Editor uses a set of styles that it cycles through for each group (category) in the chart.

▶ Select Simple Charts.

▶ Select the burgundy color, which is second from the right in the second row.

Figure 7-19
*Data Element Colors dialog box*

▶ Click Continue.

▶ In the Options dialog box, click OK to save the color style cycle changes.

The data elements in any new simple charts will now be burgundy.

▶ From the Data Editor or Viewer menus choose:
Graphs
  Bar...

▶ Click Define to open the Define Simple Bar dialog box.

▶ Deselect Use chart specifications from. If you don't deselect this option, the chart will use styles from the template rather than from the SPSS options.

▶ Click OK to create the chart.

The bars in the new chart are burgundy.

Figure 7-20
*Updated bar chart in Viewer*

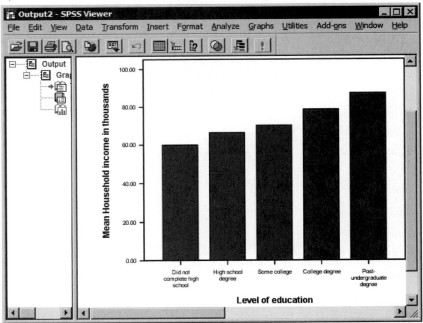

# Other Examples

Now we will create and edit a pie chart and a grouped scatterplot to explore other editing capabilities, including:

- Hiding categories
- Moving text
- Converting a chart to another chart type
- Adding a fit line to a scatterplot
- Identifying points in a scatterplot

## Pie Chart

First, we will create a simple pie chart that shows how many respondents have Internet service at home. This example uses the data file *demo.sav*.

▶ From the menus choose:
Graphs
  Pie...

▶ Click Summaries for groups of cases.

**Figure 7-21**
*Pie Charts dialog box*

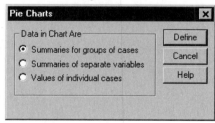

▶ Click Define.

▶ Select *Internet* as the variable that defines slices (Define Slices by).

Figure 7-22
*Define Pie dialog box*

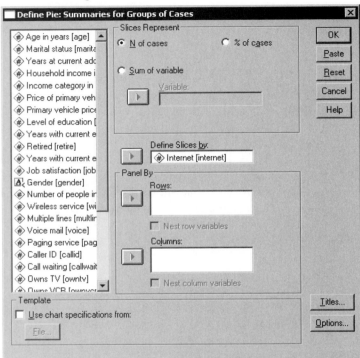

When you create charts, they do not show the *missing* category by default. You want to display this category to make sure that the number of cases with missing values is not excessive.

▶ Click Options.

▶ Select Display groups defined by missing values, and then click Continue.

**Figure 7-23**
*Options dialog box*

▶ Click OK in the Define Pie dialog box to create the pie chart.

Figure 7-24
*Pie chart in Viewer*

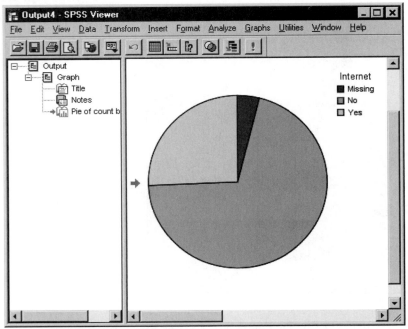

The pie chart reveals that most respondents do not have Internet service at home. From the chart, it appears that only about a quarter of the respondents have home Internet service.

For this pie chart, you will:

- Add a title.
- Remove the small category of missing data.
- Display percentages for the two remaining categories.
- Move the data labels and connect them to the slices with lines.
- Convert the pie chart to a bar chart.

▶ Double-click the pie chart to open it in the Chart Editor.

**Figure 7-25**
*Pie chart in the Chart Editor*

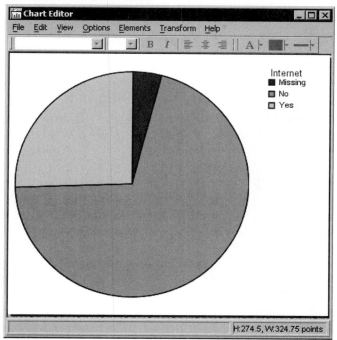

## Adding a Chart Title

First, you will add a title to the chart. Because the title applies to the entire chart and not to a specific chart element, you don't need to select anything to add the title.

▶ From the menus choose:
Options
 Title

The Chart Editor adds the word "Title" above the chart and enlarges the chart to accommodate the title. Like footnotes, the title is in a text frame that you can move to another position in the chart.

**Figure 7-26**
*Pie chart showing default title*

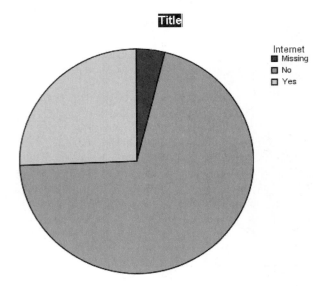

▶ Type **Home Internet Service** over the highlighted default title.

*Note*: If you clicked elsewhere in the Chart Editor, the default title may no longer be highlighted. The text frame around the title may be selected instead. If this is the case, click the title again to start edit mode. You can then double-click the title text and begin typing.

**Figure 7-27**
*Pie chart showing edited title*

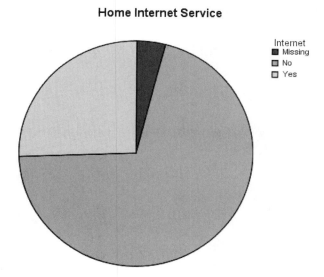

## Modifying Chart Categories

Next, you will remove the small category of missing data.

▶ In the Chart Editor, select the pie chart.

▶ Click the Categories tab in the Properties window. (If the window is closed, choose Properties from the Edit menu or press Ctrl+T.)

▶ Move *Missing* from the Order list to the Excluded list.

Figure 7-28
*Categories tab*

▶ Click Apply.

The pie chart now displays only the *No* and *Yes* categories for home Internet service.

**Figure 7-29**
*Pie chart with excluded missing category*

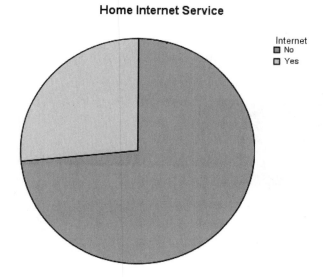

**Home Internet Service**

The pie chart clearly shows that most respondents do not have Internet service at home; it appears that about three-quarters of the respondents are in the *No* category. However, it might be useful to see the exact percentages.

### Changing Data Value Label Content and Location

▶ In the Chart Editor, select the pie chart.

▶ From the menus choose:
Elements
  Show Data Labels

The pie chart now displays labels of counts. We need to change the counts to percentages.

▶ Click the Data Value Labels tab in the Properties window.

▶ Move *Count* from the Displayed list to the Not Displayed list.

▶ Move *Percent* from the Not Displayed list to the Displayed list.

**Figure 7-30**
*Data Value Labels tab*

▶ Click Apply.

Percentages are now displayed in the pie slices.

**Figure 7-31**
*Pie chart showing percentages*

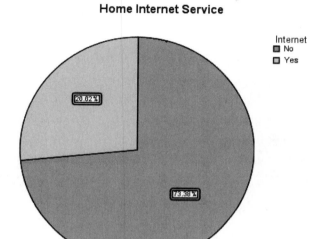

**Home Internet Service**

Internet
■ No
□ Yes

26.62%

73.38%

The percentages are based on the two categories displayed (73.4 + 26.6 = 100). If you put the category containing missing values back into the pie, the percentages will change.

You may not want the data value labels to appear in the pie slices. You can move them and add connecting lines to their respective slices.

▶ Return to the Data Value Labels tab.

▶ In the Label Position group, click Custom.

▶ Click the icon showing the labels outside the slices.

▶ Select Display connecting lines to label.

▶ Click Apply.

Data value labels now appear outside the slices with lines connecting the labels to their respective slices.

Figure 7-32
*Labels outside of pie chart*

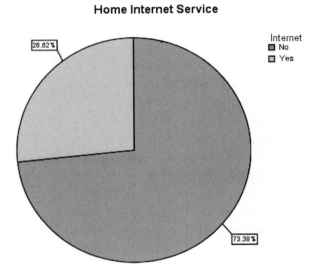

**Home Internet Service**

### Converting a Chart

Finally, you will convert the pie chart into a bar chart.

▶ From the menus choose:
Transform
  Simple Bar

The Chart Editor converts the chart and displays the result. The bar chart retains the title and data labels. However, the bars are the same color rather than the two different colors shown in the pie chart. Because the tick labels identify the categories, two colors are unnecessary.

Figure 7-33
*Bar chart converted from pie chart*

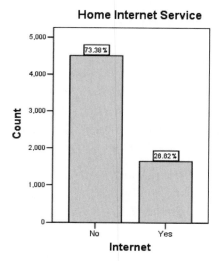

**Home Internet Service**

## Grouped Scatterplot

In this example, we will create a scatterplot using the data file *car_sales.sav*. The scatterplot will show fuel efficiency against curb weight.

▶ From the Data Editor menus choose:
Graphs
  Scatter/Dot...

▶ Click Simple Scatter.

Figure 7-34
*Scatter/Dot dialog box*

▶ Click Define.

For a scatterplot, you need to define a scale variable for each axis. Put the dependent variable on the *y* axis and the independent variable on the *x* axis.

▶ Select *Fuel efficiency* as the *y* axis variable.

▶ Select *Curb weight* as the *x* axis variable.

▶ Select *Vehicle type* as the grouping variable (Set Markers by).

Figure 7-35
*Simple Scatterplot dialog box*

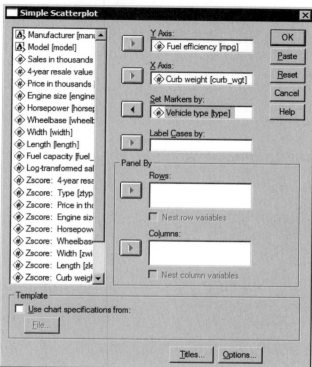

▶ Click OK.

▶ In the Viewer, double-click the resulting scatterplot to display it in the Chart Editor.

**Figure 7-36**
*Scatterplot in the Chart Editor*

## Selecting Elements in Grouped Charts

Selecting an element in grouped charts (that is, charts with categories) differs from selecting an element in simple charts. You can tell that a chart is grouped because it includes, by default, a legend for the groups.

You can hide the legend if necessary (choose Hide Legend from the Options menu). However, the legend provides important information for interpreting the chart. You can also use the legend to easily select groups.

There are general rules for selecting elements in grouped charts:

- When no data elements are selected, click any data element to select all data elements.

- When all data elements are selected, click a data element in a specific group to select all data elements in the group. You can then click a data element in another group to select its associated group.

- You can also click the legend entry for a group to select only that group.

- When a group of data elements is selected, click a data element in the group to select only that data element. You can then select another data element in the chart by clicking it.

With specific data elements selected, you can make changes to only the selected data elements. So, you could change the color of data elements in a group. In this example, we changed the fill color of the marker from transparent to the same color as its border.

**Figure 7-37**
*Scatterplot showing one case with a different fill color*

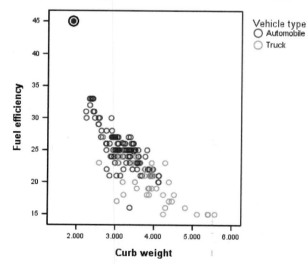

### Adding a Fit Line

With scatterplots, you often want to add a fit line to the chart. For elements like fit lines that apply to the whole chart, it doesn't matter what is selected in the chart. You can make the change or add the item to the whole chart. If you were creating a fit line for only one or more specific groups, you would need to make specific selections.

▶ From the menus choose:
Elements
  Fit Line at Total

Figure 7-38
*Scatterplot showing fit line at total*

The Chart Editor adds the fit line to the chart. It also displays the coefficient of determination, $R^2$. $R^2$ is the proportion of the variability in the dependent variable (*y* axis) that can be explained by the independent variable (*x* axis). In this example, we can say that 67% of the variability in *Fuel efficiency* values can be explained by *Curb weight*. The closer $R^2$ is to 1, the better the line fits the data.

### *Displaying Data Value Labels for Specific Points*

Previously, in the bar and pie chart examples, we displayed the data value labels for all data elements. With scatterplots, displaying data value labels for all markers is not usually useful. There are too many data elements, making viewing of the associated data value labels difficult.

▶ For example, from the menus choose:
Elements
  Show Data Labels

The results are cluttered and of limited use.

Figure 7-39
*Scatterplot showing all data value labels*

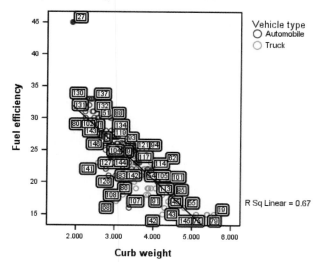

Not every marker in the scatterplot has a displayed data value label. This occurs because of a Data Value Labels tab setting that suppresses overlapping labels. This setting helps to eliminate some of the clutter, but you don't have control over which particular data value labels are displayed. You could turn off this setting to display all data value labels, even the overlapping ones. However, many labels would become unreadable. A better option would be to display data value labels for only those points that you want to highlight.

First, hide the current data value labels.

▶ From the menus choose:
Elements
  Hide Data Labels

Next, turn on data label mode, which allows you to click any data element and automatically display its data value label.

▶ From the menus choose:
Elements
  Data Label Mode

The cursor changes to indicate that you are in data label mode.

▶ Click the marker for which we previously changed the fill color.

Figure 7-40
*Scatterplot with one marker showing a data value label*

The Chart Editor now displays the data value label for only that marker. You can repeat this process for each marker that needs a data value label. You can also hide a data value label by clicking it while in data label mode.

The data value label contains the case number. You can change the contents of the data value label on the Data Value Labels tab.

▶ When you are finished labeling the data elements, exit data label mode. From the menus choose:

Elements
  Data Label Mode

# *Working with Syntax*

SPSS syntax provides a method for you to control the product without navigating through dialog boxes, viewers, or data editors. Instead, you control the application through syntax-based commands. Nearly every action you can achieve through the user interface can be achieved through syntax. Using syntax also allows you to save the exact specifications used during a session. Syntax is not available with the Student Version.

The examples in this chapter use the data file *demo.sav*.

## *Pasting Syntax*

The easiest way to create syntax is to use the Paste button located on most dialog boxes.

▶ Open *demo.sav* for use in this example.

▶ From the menus choose:
Analyze
  Descriptive Statistics
    Frequencies...

This opens the Frequencies dialog box.

**Figure 8-1**
*Frequencies dialog box*

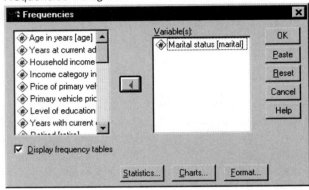

▶ Select *Marital status (marital)* in the source list.

▶ Click the arrow button to move the variable to the Variables list.

▶ Click Charts.

▶ In the Charts dialog box, select Bar charts.

▶ In the Chart Values group, select Percentages.

▶ Click Continue.

▶ Click Paste to copy the syntax created as a result of the dialog box selections to the Syntax Editor.

Figure 8-2
*Frequencies syntax*

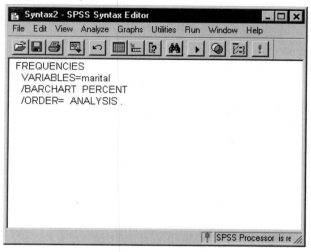

You can use this syntax alone, add it to a larger syntax file, or refer to it in a
Production Facility job.

▶ To run the syntax currently displayed, from the menus choose:
Run
  Current

## *Editing Syntax*

In the syntax window, you can edit the syntax. For example, you could change the subcommand /BARCHART to display frequencies instead of percentages. (A subcommand is indicated by a slash.)

**Figure 8-3**
*Modified syntax*

To find out what subcommands and keywords are available for the current command, click the Syntax Help button. The example shows the complete syntax for the FREQUENCIES command.

Figure 8-4
*FREQUENCIES syntax help*

If the cursor is not in a command, clicking the Syntax Help button displays an alphabetical list of commands. You can select the one you want.

# *Typing Syntax*

You can type syntax into a syntax window that is already open, or you can open a new syntax window by choosing:

File
  New
    Syntax...

# Saving Syntax

To save a syntax file, from the menus choose:

File
  Save

*or*

File
  Save As...

Either action opens the standard dialog box for saving files.

# Opening and Running a Syntax File

▶ To open a saved syntax file, from the menus choose:

File
  Open
    Syntax...

▶ Select a syntax file. If no syntax files are displayed, make sure Syntax (*.sps) is selected in the Files of type drop-down list.

▶ Click Open.

▶ To run the syntax currently displayed, from the menus choose:

Run
  Current

If the commands apply to a specific data file, the data file must be opened before running the commands, or you must include a command that opens the data file. You can paste this type of command from the dialog boxes that open data files.

# Modifying Data Values

The data you start with may not always be organized in the most useful manner for your analysis or reporting needs. For example, you may want to:

- Create a categorical variable from a scale variable.

- Combine several response categories into a single category.

- Create a new variable that is the computed difference between two existing variables.

This chapter uses the data file *demo.sav*.

## Creating a Categorical Variable from a Scale Variable

Several categorical variables in the data file *demo.sav* are, in fact, derived from scale variables in that data file. For example, the variable *inccat* is simply *income* grouped into four categories. This categorical variable uses the integer values 1–4 to represent the following income categories: less than 25, 25–49, 50–74, and 75 or higher.

To create the categorical variable *inccat*:

▶ From the menus in the Data Editor window choose:
Transform
  Visual Bander...

Figure 9-1
*Initial Visual Bander dialog box*

In the initial Visual Bander dialog box, you select the scale and/or ordinal variables for which you want to create new, banded variables. **Banding** means taking two or more contiguous values and grouping them into the same category.

Since the Visual Bander relies on actual values in the data file to help you make good banding choices, it needs to read the data file first. Since this can take some time if your data file contains a large number of cases, this initial dialog box also allows you to limit the number of cases to read ("scan"). This is not necessary for our sample data file. Even though it contains more than 6,000 cases, it does not take long to scan that number of cases.

▶ Drag and drop *Household income in thousands [income]* from the Variables list into the Variables to Band list, and then click Continue.

**Figure 9-2**
*Main Visual Bander dialog box*

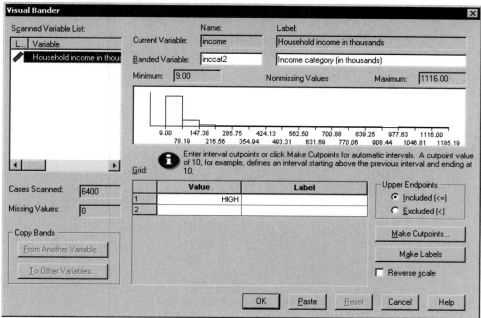

► In the main Visual Bander dialog box, select *Household income in thousands [income]* in the Scanned Variable List.

A histogram displays the distribution of the selected variable (which in this case is highly skewed).

► Enter inccat2 for the new banded variable name and Income category (in thousands) for the variable label.

► Click Make Cutpoints.

Figure 9-3
*Visual Bander Cutpoints dialog box*

▶ Select Equal Width Intervals.

▶ Enter 25 for the first cutpoint location, 3 for the number of cutpoints, and 25 for the width.

The number of banded categories is one greater than the number of cutpoints. So, in this example, the new banded variable will have four categories, with the first three categories each containing ranges of 25 (thousand) and the last one containing all values above the highest cutpoint value of 75 (thousand).

▶ Click Apply.

**Figure 9-4**
*Main Visual Bander dialog box with defined cutpoints*

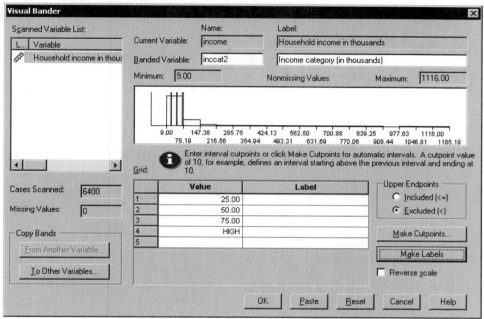

The values now displayed in the grid represent the defined cutpoints, which are the upper endpoints of each category. Vertical lines in the histogram also indicate the locations of the cutpoints.

By default, these cutpoint values are included in the corresponding categories. For example, the first value of 25 would include all values less than or equal to 25. But in this example, we want categories that correspond to less than 25, 25–49, 50–74, and 75 or higher.

▶ In the Upper Endpoints group, select Excluded (<).

▶ Then click Make Labels.

**Figure 9-5**
*Automatically generated value labels*

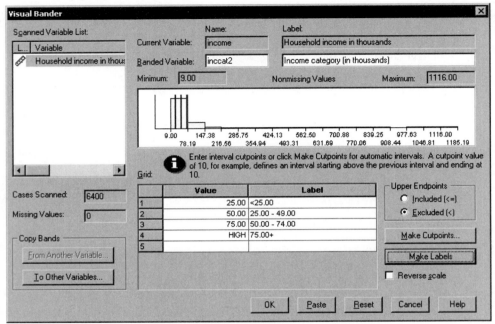

This automatically generates descriptive value labels for each category. Since the actual values assigned to the new banded variable are simply sequential integers starting with 1, the value labels can be very useful.

You can also manually enter or change cutpoints and labels in the grid, change cutpoint locations by dragging and dropping the cutpoint lines in the histogram, and delete cutpoints by dragging cutpoint lines off of the histogram.

▶ Click OK to create the new, banded variable.

The new variable is displayed in the Data Editor. Since the variable is added to the end of the file, it is displayed in the far right column in Data View and in the last row in Variable View.

Figure 9-6
*New variable displayed in Data Editor*

## Computing New Variables

Using a wide variety of mathematical functions, you can compute new variables based on highly complex equations. In this example, however, we will simply compute a new variable that is the difference between the values of two existing variables.

The data file *demo.sav* contains a variable for the respondent's current age and a variable for the number of years at current job. It does not, however, contain a variable for the respondent's age at the time he or she started that job. We can create a new variable that is the computed difference between current age and number of years at current job, which should be the approximate age at which the respondent started that job.

▶ From the menus in the Data Editor window choose:

Transform
  Compute...

▶ For Target Variable, enter jobstart.

▶ Select *Age in years (age)* in the source variable list and click the arrow button to copy it to the Numeric Expression text box.

▶ Click the minus (–) button on the calculator pad in the dialog box (or press the minus key on the keyboard).

▶ Select *Years with current employer (employ)* and click the arrow button to copy it to the expression.

Figure 9-7
*Compute Variable dialog box*

*Note*: Be careful to select the correct employment variable. There is also a recoded categorical version of the variable, which is *not* what you want. The numeric expression should be *age-employ*, not *age-empcat*.

▶ Click OK to compute the new variable.

The new variable is displayed in the Data Editor. Since the variable is added to the end of the file, it is displayed in the far right column in Data View and in the last row in Variable View.

Figure 9-8
*New variable displayed in the Data Editor*

## Using Functions in Expressions

You can also use predefined functions in expressions. More than 70 built-in functions are available, including:

- Arithmetic functions
- Statistical functions
- Distribution functions
- Logical functions

- Date and time aggregation and extraction functions
- Missing-value functions
- Cross-case functions
- String functions

**Figure 9-9**
*Compute Variable dialog box displaying function grouping*

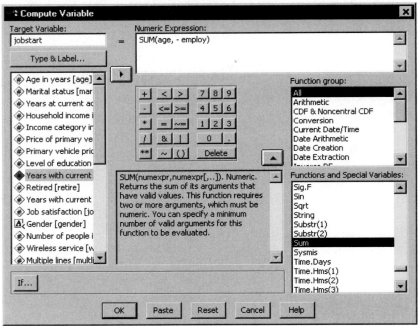

Functions are organized into logically distinct groups, such as a group for arithmetic operations and another for computing statistical metrics. For convenience, a number of commonly used system variables, such as *$TIME* (current date and time), are also included in appropriate function groups. A brief description of the currently selected function (in this case, SUM) or system variable is displayed in a reserved area in the Compute Variable dialog box.

**Pasting a function into an expression.** To paste a function into an expression:

▶ Position the cursor in the expression at the point where you want the function to appear.

▶ Select the appropriate group from the Function group list. The group labeled All provides a listing of all available functions and system variables.

▶ Double-click the function in the Functions and Special Variables list (or select the function and click the arrow adjacent to the Function group list).

The function is inserted into the expression. If you highlight part of the expression and then insert the function, the highlighted portion of the expression is used as the first argument in the function.

**Editing a function in an expression.** The function is not complete until you enter the arguments, represented by question marks in the pasted function. The number of question marks indicates the minimum number of arguments required to complete the function.

▶ Highlight the question mark(s) in the pasted function.

▶ Enter the arguments. If the arguments are variable names, you can paste them from the variable list.


## Using Conditional Expressions

You can use conditional expressions (also called logical expressions) to apply transformations to selected subsets of cases. A conditional expression returns a value of true, false, or missing for each case. If the result of a conditional expression is true, the transformation is applied to that case. If the result is false or missing, the transformation is not applied to the case.

To specify a conditional expression:

▶ Click If in the Compute Variable dialog box. This opens the If Cases dialog box.

**Figure 9-10**
*If Cases dialog box*

▶ Select Include if case satisfies condition.

▶ Enter the conditional expression.

Most conditional expressions contain at least one relational operator, as in:

`age>=21`

*or*

`income*3<100`

In the first example, only cases with a value of 21 or greater for *Age (age)* are selected. In the second example, *Household income in thousands (income)* multiplied by 3 must be less than 100 for a case to be selected.

You can also link two or more conditional expressions using logical operators, as in:

```
age>=21 | ed>=4
```

*or*

```
income*3<100 & ed=5
```

In the first example, cases that meet either the *Age (age)* condition or the *Level of education (ed)* condition are selected. In the second example, both the *Household income in thousands (income)* and *Level of education (ed)* conditions must be met for a case to be selected.

## Computing Variables with Missing Values

When computing variables with missing values, it's a good idea to perform a trial on a small data file in order to ensure that your missing data are handled in a way that is acceptable. Some computations handle missing data by removing them from the equation, while others cannot perform the computation and the new value is considered missing. The following examples use *car_sales.sav*.

There are two different ways to compute the mean of a set of variables. The first is to divide the sum of the set of variables by the number of variables in the set.

▶ From the menus choose:
Transform
    Compute...

▶ Type avgsale in the Target Variable text box.

▶ Type (resale + price) / 2 in the Numeric Expression text box.

**Figure 9-11**
*Find the average*

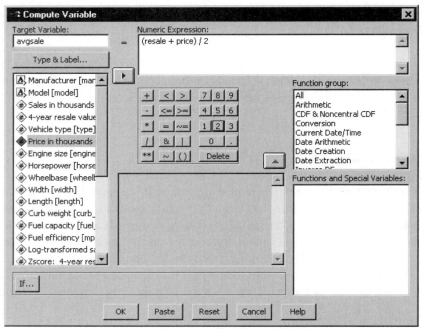

This equation finds the average of the original price of a car and its four-year resale price.

▶ Click OK.

A new variable has been added to the end of the data file. This variable, which we named *avgsale*, is in the far right column in Data View. Any cases that have missing values in either of the two variables that we computed also have a missing value for the *avgsale* variable.

Figure 9-12
*Data Editor with avgsale added*

| | zcurb_wg | zfuel_ca | zmpg | avgsale | var | var | var |
|---|---|---|---|---|---|---|---|
| 1 | -1.17212 | -1.22223 | .97053 | 18.93 | | | |
| 2 | .22042 | -.19340 | .27004 | 24.14 | | | |
| 3 | .14587 | -.19340 | .50353 | . | | | |
| 4 | .74857 | .01237 | -.43045 | 35.86 | | | |
| 5 | -.60274 | -.39917 | .73703 | 23.12 | | | |
| 6 | .29020 | .14097 | -.43045 | 28.75 | | | |
| 7 | .83104 | 1.47844 | -.66395 | 50.50 | | | |
| 8 | -.31566 | -.34772 | .52688 | . | | | |
| 9 | -.28711 | -.34772 | .03654 | 31.04 | | | |
| 10 | .14905 | .14097 | .22334 | 37.51 | | | |
| 11 | -.01590 | -.11624 | .27004 | 17.23 | | | |
| 12 | .26166 | -.11624 | -.19696 | 19.52 | | | |
| 13 | .63437 | .14097 | .03654 | 26.08 | | | |
| 14 | .33779 | -.11624 | .27004 | 20.62 | | | |
| 15 | .95158 | .14097 | -.43045 | 31.21 | | | |

The second way to compute the mean of a set of variables is to use the mean function.

▶ Recall the Compute Variable dialog box.

▶ Click Reset to clear the previous selections in this dialog box.

▶ Type meansale in the Target Variable text box.

▶ Type mean(resale, price) in the Numeric Expression text box.

**Figure 9-13**
*Find the mean*

Like the previous example, this equation finds the average, or mean, of the car's original price and its four-year resale price.

▶ Click OK.

The *meansale* variable is added to the far right column in Data View. Unlike the previous example, the mean function removes missing values from the equation and computes the mean of the remaining values. You can modify the behavior of this function to limit the number of values that can be removed from the equation.

Figure 9-14
*Results from two mean calculations*

| | zcurb_wg | zfuel_ca | zmpg | avgsale | meansale | var | var |
|---|---|---|---|---|---|---|---|
| 1 | -1.17212 | -1.22223 | .97053 | 18.93 | 18.93 | | |
| 2 | .22042 | -.19340 | .27004 | 24.14 | 24.14 | | |
| 3 | .14587 | -.19340 | .50353 | . | 18.23 | | |
| 4 | .74857 | .01237 | -.43045 | 35.86 | 35.86 | | |
| 5 | -.60274 | -.39917 | .73703 | 23.12 | 23.12 | | |
| 6 | .29020 | .14097 | -.43045 | 28.75 | 28.75 | | |
| 7 | .83104 | 1.47844 | -.66395 | 50.50 | 50.50 | | |
| 8 | -.31566 | -.34772 | .52688 | . | 26.99 | | |
| 9 | -.28711 | -.34772 | .03654 | 31.04 | 31.04 | | |
| 10 | .14905 | .14097 | .22334 | 37.51 | 37.51 | | |
| 11 | -.01590 | -.11624 | .27004 | 17.23 | 17.23 | | |
| 12 | .26166 | -.11624 | -.19696 | 19.52 | 19.52 | | |
| 13 | .63437 | .14097 | .03654 | 26.08 | 26.08 | | |
| 14 | .33779 | -.11624 | .27004 | 20.62 | 20.62 | | |
| 15 | .95158 | .14097 | -.43045 | 31.21 | 31.21 | | |

If you want to find the mean of four variables and only want a result if three or more of the variables have valid values, you could use the following syntax:

```
newvar = mean.3(var1, var2, var3, var4)
```

Figure 9-15
*Specifying number of valid values for mean calculation*

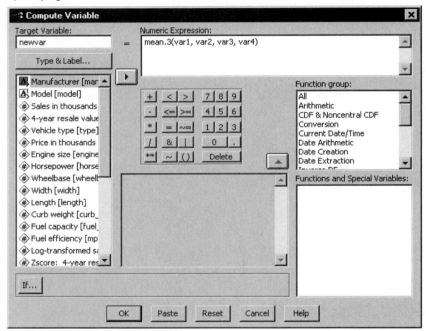

To raise or lower the number of required valid values, simply change the number following mean (which is 3 in this example).

# Sorting and Selecting Data

Data files are not always organized in the ideal form for your specific needs. To prepare data for analysis, you can select from a wide range of file transformations, including the ability to:

- **Sort data.** You can sort cases based on the value of one or more variables.

- **Select subsets of cases.** You can restrict your analysis to a subset of cases or perform simultaneous analyses on different subsets.

The examples in this chapter use the data file *demo.sav*.

## Sorting Data

Sorting cases (sorting rows of the data file) is often useful and sometimes necessary for certain types of analysis.

To reorder the sequence of cases in the data file based on the value of one or more sorting variables:

▶ From the menus choose:
Data
    Sort Cases...

This opens the Sort Cases dialog box.

**Figure 10-1**
*Sort Cases dialog box*

▶ Add the *Age in years (age)* and *Household income in thousands (income)* variables to the Sort By list.

If you select multiple sort variables, the order in which they appear on the Sort By list determines the order in which cases are sorted. In this example, based on the entries in the Sort By list, cases will be sorted by the value of *Household income in thousands (income)* within categories of *Age in years (age)*. For string variables, uppercase letters precede their lowercase counterparts in sort order (for example, the string value *Yes* comes before *yes* in the sort order).

# Split-File Processing

To split your data file into separate groups for analysis:

▶ From the menus choose:
Data
    Split File...

This opens the Split File dialog box.

Figure 10-2
*Split File dialog box*

▶ Select Compare groups or Organize output by groups. The examples following these steps show the differences between these two options.

▶ Select *Gender (gender)* to split the file into separate groups for these variables.

You can use numeric, short string, and long string variables as grouping variables. A separate analysis is performed for each subgroup defined by the grouping variables. If you select multiple grouping variables, the order in which they appear on the Groups Based On list determines the manner in which cases are grouped.

If you select Compare groups and run the Frequencies procedure, a single pivot table is created.

**Figure 10-3**
*Split File output with single pivot table*

**Statistics**

Household income in thousands

| | | | |
|---|---|---|---|
| Female | N | Valid | 3179 |
| | | Missing | 0 |
| | Mean | | 68.7798 |
| | Median | | 44.0000 |
| | Std. Deviation | | 75.73510 |
| Male | N | Valid | 3221 |
| | | Missing | 0 |
| | Mean | | 70.1608 |
| | Median | | 45.0000 |
| | Std. Deviation | | 81.56216 |

If you select Organize output by groups and run the Frequencies procedure, two pivot tables are created: one for females and one for males.

**Figure 10-4**
*Split File output with pivot table for females*

**Statistics**[a]

Household income in thousands

| | | |
|---|---|---|
| N | Valid | 3179 |
| | Missing | 0 |
| Mean | | 68.7798 |
| Median | | 44.0000 |
| Std. Deviation | | 75.73510 |

a. Gender = Female

Figure 10-5
*Split File output with pivot table for males*

**Statistics**ᵃ

Household income in thousands

| N | Valid | 3221 |
|---|---|---|
| | Missing | 0 |
| Mean | | 70.1608 |
| Median | | 45.0000 |
| Std. Deviation | | 81.56216 |

a. Gender = Male

## Sorting Cases for Split-File Processing

The Split File procedure creates a new subgroup each time it encounters a different value for one of the grouping variables. Therefore, it is important to sort cases based on the values of the grouping variables before invoking split-file processing.

By default, Split File automatically sorts the data file based on the values of the grouping variables. If the file is already sorted in the proper order, you can save processing time if you select File is already sorted.

## Turning Split-File Processing On and Off

Once you invoke split-file processing, it remains in effect for the rest of the session unless you turn it off.

■ **Analyze all cases.** Turns split-file processing off.

■ **Compare groups** and **Organize output by groups.** Turns split-file processing on.

If split-file processing is in effect, the message Split File on appears on the status bar at the bottom of the application window.

# Selecting Subsets of Cases

You can restrict your analysis to a specific subgroup based on criteria that include variables and complex expressions. You can also select a random sample of cases. The criteria used to define a subgroup can include:

- Variable values and ranges
- Date and time ranges
- Case (row) numbers
- Arithmetic expressions
- Logical expressions
- Functions

To select a subset of cases for analysis:

▶ From the menus choose:
Data
  Select Cases...

This opens the Select Cases dialog box.

**Figure 10-6**
*Select Cases dialog box*

## Selecting Cases Based on Conditional Expressions

To select cases based on a conditional expression:

▶ Select If condition is satisfied and click If in the Select Cases dialog box.

This opens the Select Cases If dialog box.

**Figure 10-7**
*Select Cases If dialog box*

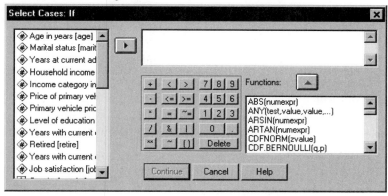

The conditional expression can use existing variable names, constants, arithmetic operators, logical operators, relational operators, and functions. You can type and edit the expression in the text box just like text in an output window. You can also use the calculator pad, variable list, and function list to paste elements into the expression. For more information, see "Using Conditional Expressions" in Chapter 9 on p. 187.

## Selecting a Random Sample

To obtain a random sample:

▶ Select Random sample of cases in the Select Cases dialog box.

▶ Click Sample.

This opens the Select Cases Random Sample dialog box.

Figure 10-8
*Select Cases Random Sample dialog box*

You can select one of the following alternatives for sample size:

■ **Approximately.** A user-specified percentage. This option generates a random sample of approximately the specified percentage of cases.

■ **Exactly.** A user-specified number of cases. You must also specify the number of cases from which to generate the sample. This second number should be less than or equal to the total number of cases in the data file. If the number exceeds the total number of cases in the data file, the sample will contain proportionally fewer cases than the requested number.

## Selecting a Time Range or Case Range

To select a range of cases based on dates, times, or observation (row) numbers:

▶ Select Based on time or case range and click Range in the Select Cases dialog box.

This opens the Select Cases Range dialog box, in which you can select a range of observation (row) numbers.

Figure 10-9
*Select Cases Range dialog box*

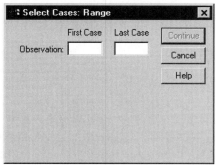

- **First Case.** Enter the starting date and/or time values for the range. If no date variables are defined, enter the starting observation number (row number in the Data Editor, unless Split File is on). If you do not specify a Last Case value, all cases from the starting date/time to the end of the time series are selected.

- **Last Case.** Enter the ending date and/or time values for the range. If no date variables are defined, enter the ending observation number (row number in the Data Editor, unless Split File is on). If you do not specify a First Case value, all cases from the beginning of the time series up to the ending date/time are selected.

For time series data with defined date variables, you can select a range of dates and/or times based on the defined date variables. Each case represents observations at a different time, and the file is sorted in chronological order.

Figure 10-10
*Select Cases Range dialog box (time series)*

To generate date variables for time series data:

▶ From the menus choose:
Data
    Define Dates...

## Unselected Cases

You can choose one of the following alternatives for the treatment of unselected cases:

- **Filtered.** Unselected cases are not included in the analysis but remain in the data file. You can use the unselected cases later in the session if you turn filtering off. If you select a random sample or if you select cases based on a conditional expression, this generates a variable named *filter_$* with a value of 1 for selected cases and a value of 0 for unselected cases.

- **Deleted.** Unselected cases are deleted from the data file. By reducing the number of cases in the open data file, you can save processing time. Deleted cases can be recovered only by exiting from the file without saving any changes and then reopening the file. The deletion of cases is permanent if you save the changes to the data file. *Note*: If you delete unselected cases and save the file, the cases cannot be recovered.

## Case Selection Status

If you have selected a subset of cases but have not discarded unselected cases, unselected cases are marked in the Data Editor with a diagonal line through the row number.

Figure 10-11
*Case selection status*

# *Additional Statistical Procedures*

This chapter contains brief examples for selected statistical procedures. The procedures are grouped according to the order in which they appear on the Analyze menu.

The examples are designed to illustrate sample specifications required to run a statistical procedure. The examples in this chapter use the data file *demo.sav*, except for the following:

- The paired-samples *t* test example uses the data file *dietstudy.sav*, which is a hypothetical data file containing the results of a study of the "Stillman diet." In the examples in this chapter, you must run the procedures to see the output.

- The correlation examples use *Employee data.sav*, which contains historical data about a company's employees.

- The exponential smoothing example uses the data file *inventor.sav*, which contains inventory data collected over a period of 70 days.

For information about individual items in a dialog box, click Help. If you want to locate a specific statistic, such as percentiles, use the Index or Search facility in the Help system. For additional information about interpreting the results obtained by running these procedures, consult a statistics or data analysis textbook.

## *Summarizing Data*

The Descriptive Statistics submenu on the Analyze menu provides techniques for summarizing data with statistics and charts.

# *Frequencies*

In the chapter *Examining Summary Statistics for Individual Variables*, there is an example showing a frequency table and a bar chart. In that example, the Frequencies procedure was used to analyze the variables *Owns PDA (ownpda)* and *Owns TV (owntv)*, both of which are categorical variables having only two values. If the variable that you want to analyze is a scale (interval, ratio) variable, you can use the Frequencies procedure to generate summary statistics and a histogram. A **histogram** is a chart that shows the number of cases in each of several groups. This example will use Frequencies to analyze the variable *Years with current employer (employ)*.

To generate statistics and a histogram of the years with current employer, follow these steps:

▶ From the menus choose:
Analyze
  Descriptive Statistics
    Frequencies...

This opens the Frequencies dialog box.

**Figure 11-1**
*Frequencies dialog box*

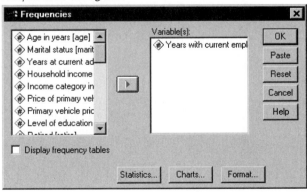

▶ Select *Years with current employer (employ)* and move it to the Variable(s) list.

▶ Deselect the Display frequency tables check box.

(If you leave this item selected and display a frequency table for current salary, the output shows an entry for every distinct value of salary, making a very long table.)

▶ Click Charts to open the Frequencies Charts dialog box.

Figure 11-2
*Frequencies Charts dialog box*

▶ Select Histograms and With normal curve, and then click Continue.

▶ To select summary statistics, click Statistics in the Frequencies dialog box. This displays the Frequencies Statistics dialog box.

Figure 11-3
*Frequencies Statistics dialog box*

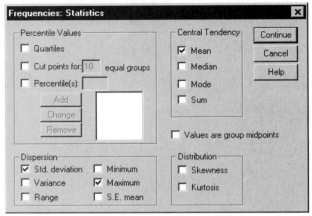

▶ Select Mean, Std. deviation, and Maximum, and then click Continue.

▶ Click OK in the Frequencies dialog box to run the procedure.

The Viewer shows the requested statistics and a histogram in standard graphics format. Each bar in the histogram represents the number of employees within a range of five years, and the year values displayed are the range midpoints. As requested, a normal curve is superimposed on the chart.

## Explore

Suppose that you want to look further at the distribution of the years with current employer for each income category. With the Explore procedure, you can examine the distribution of the years with current employer within categories of another variable.

▶ From the menus choose:

Analyze
  Descriptive Statistics
    Explore...

This opens the Explore dialog box.

**Figure 11-4**
*Explore dialog box*

▶ Select *Years with current employer (employ)* and move it to the Dependent List.

▶ Select *Income category in thousands (inccat)* and move it to the Factor List.

▶ Click OK to run the Explore procedure.

In the output, descriptive statistics and a stem-and-leaf plot are displayed for the years with current employer in each income category. The Viewer also contains a boxplot (in standard graphics format) comparing the years with current employer in the income categories. For each category, the boxplot shows the median, interquartile range (25th to 75th percentile), outliers (indicated by O), and extreme values (indicated by *).

## *More about Summarizing Data*

There are many ways to summarize data. For example, to calculate medians or percentiles, use the Frequencies procedure or the Explore procedure. Here are some additional methods:

- **Descriptives.** For income, you can calculate standard scores, sometimes called *z* scores. Use the Descriptives procedure and select Save standardized values as variables.

- **Crosstabs.** You can use the Crosstabs procedure to display the relationship between two or more categorical variables.

- **Summarize procedure.** You can use the Summarize procedure to write to your output window a listing of the actual values of age, gender, and income of the first 25 or 50 cases.

To run the Summarize procedure, from the menus choose:

Analyze
  Reports
    Case Summaries...

# *Comparing Means*

The Compare Means submenu on the Analyze menu provides techniques for displaying descriptive statistics and testing whether differences are significant between two means for both independent and paired samples. You can also test whether differences are significant among more than two independent means by using the One-Way ANOVA procedure.

## *Means*

In the *demo.sav* file, several variables are available for dividing people into groups. You can then calculate various statistics in order to compare the groups. For example, you can compute the average (mean) household income for males and females. To calculate the means, use the following steps:

▶ From the menus choose:

Analyze
  Compare Means
    Means...

This opens the Means dialog box.

**Figure 11-5**
*Means dialog box (layer 1)*

▶ Select *Household income in thousands (income)* and move it to the Dependent List.

▶ Select *Gender (gender)* and move it to the Independent List in layer 1.

▶ Click Next. This creates another layer.

**Figure 11-6**
*Means dialog box (layer 2)*

▶ Select *Owns PDA (ownpda)* and move it to the Independent List in layer 2.

▶ Click OK to run the procedure.

## Paired-Samples T Test

When the data are structured in such a way that there are two observations on the same individual or observations that are matched by another variable on two individuals (twins, for example), the samples are paired. In the data file *dietstudy.sav*, the beginning and final weights are provided for each person who participated in the study. If the diet worked, we expect that the participant's weight before and after the study would be significantly different.

To carry out a *t* test of the beginning and final weights, use the following steps:

▶ Open the data file *dietstudy.sav*, which can be found in the *\tutorial\sample_files\* subdirectory of the directory in which you installed SPSS.

▶ From the menus choose:

Analyze
  Compare Means
    Paired-Samples T Test...

This opens the Paired-Samples T Test dialog box.

**Figure 11-7**
*Paired-Samples T Test dialog box*

▶ Click *Weight (wgt0)*. The variable is displayed in the Current Selections group (below the variable list).

▶ Click *Final weight (wgt4)*. The variable is displayed in the Current Selections group.

▶ Click the arrow button to move the pair to the Paired Variables list.

▶ Click OK to run the procedure. If there are rows of asterisks in some columns, double-click the chart and drag to make the columns wider.

The results show that the final weight is significantly different from the beginning weight, as indicated by the small probability displayed in the *Sig. (2-tailed)* column of the Paired Samples Test table.

## More about Comparing Means

The following examples suggest some ways in which you can use other procedures to compare means.

- **Independent-Samples T Test.** When you use a *t* test to compare means of one variable across independent groups, the samples are independent. Males and females in the *demo.sav* file can be divided into independent groups by the variable *Gender (gender)*. You can use a *t* test to determine if the mean household incomes of males and females are the same.

- **One-Sample T Test.** You can test whether the household income of people with college degrees differs from a national or state average. Use Select Cases on the Data menu to select the cases with *Level of Education (ed)* >= 4. Then, run the One-Sample T Test procedure to compare *Household income in thousands (income)* and the test value 75.

- **One-Way ANOVA.** The variable *Level of Education (ed)* divides employees into five independent groups by level of education. You can use the One-Way ANOVA procedure to test whether *Household income in thousands (income)* means for the five groups are significantly different.

# ANOVA Models

The General Linear Model submenu on the Analyze menu provides techniques for testing univariate analysis-of-variance models. (If you have only one factor, you can use the One-Way ANOVA procedure on the Compare Means submenu.)

## Univariate Analysis of Variance

The GLM Univariate procedure can perform an analysis of variance for factorial designs. A simple factorial design can be used to test if a person's household income and job satisfaction affect the number of years with current employer.

► From the menus choose:

Analyze
  General Linear Model
    Univariate...

This opens the Univariate dialog box.

**Figure 11-8**
*Univariate dialog box*

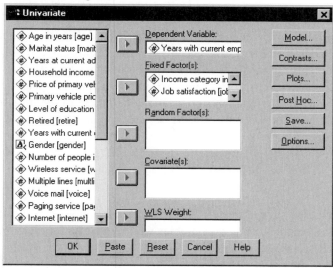

► Select *Years with current employer (employ)* as the dependent variable.

► Select *Income category in thousands (inccat)* and *Job satisfaction (jobsat)* as fixed factors.

► Click OK to run the procedure.

In the Tests of Between-Subjects Effects table, you can see that the effects of income and job satisfaction are definitely significant and that the observed significance level of the interaction of income and job satisfaction is 0.000. For further interpretation, consult a statistics or data analysis textbook.

# Correlating Variables

The Correlate submenu on the Analyze menu provides measures of association for two or more numeric variables.

The examples in this topic use the data file *Employee data.sav*.

## Bivariate Correlations

The Bivariate Correlations procedure computes statistics such as Pearson's correlation coefficient. Correlations measure how variables or rank orders are related. Correlation coefficients range in value from –1 (a perfect negative relationship) and +1 (a perfect positive relationship). A value of 0 indicates no linear relationship.

For example, you can use Pearson's correlation coefficient to see if there is a strong linear association between *Current Salary (salary)* and *Beginning Salary (salbegin)* in the data file *Employee data.sav*.

## Partial Correlations

The Partial Correlations procedure calculates partial correlation coefficients that describe the relationship between two variables while adjusting for the effects of one or more additional variables.

You can estimate the correlation between *Current Salary (salary)* and *Beginning Salary (salbegin)*, controlling for the linear effects of *Months since Hire (jobtime)* and *Previous Experience (prevexp)*. The number of control variables determines the order of the partial correlation coefficient.

To carry out this Partial Correlations procedure, use the following steps:

▶ Open the *Employee data.sav* file. It is usually in the directory where SPSS is installed.

▶ From the menus choose:

Analyze
  Correlate
    Partial...

This opens the Partial Correlations dialog box.

**Figure 11-9**
*Partial Correlations dialog box*

▶ Select *Current Salary (salary)* and *Beginning Salary (salbegin)* and move them to the Variables list.

▶ Select *Months since Hire (jobtime)* and *Previous Experience (prevexp)* and move them to the Controlling For list.

▶ Click OK to run the procedure.

The output shows a table of partial correlation coefficients, the degrees of freedom, and the significance level for the pair *Current Salary (salary)* and *Beginning Salary (salbegin)*.

# Regression Analysis

The Regression submenu on the Analyze menu provides regression techniques.

## Linear Regression

The Linear Regression procedure examines the relationship between a dependent variable and a set of independent variables. You can use it to predict a person's household income (the dependent variable) from independent variables such as age, number in household, and years with employer.

▶ From the menus choose:

Analyze
  Regression
    Linear...

This opens the Linear Regression dialog box.

Figure 11-10
*Linear Regression dialog box*

▶ Select *Household income in thousands (income)* and move it to the Dependent list.

▶ Select *Age in years (age)*, *Number of people in household (reside)*, and *Years with current employer (employ)* and move them to the Independent(s) list.

▶ Click OK to run the procedure.

The output contains goodness-of-fit statistics and the partial regression coefficients for the variables.

**Examining fit.** To see how well the regression model fits your data, you can examine the residuals and other types of diagnostics that this procedure provides. In the Linear Regression dialog box, click Save to see a list of the new variables that you can add to your data file. If you generate any of these variables, they will not be available in a later session unless you save the data file.

**Methods.** If you have collected a large number of independent variables and want to build a regression model that includes only variables that are statistically related to the dependent variable, you can select a method from the drop-down list. For example, if you select Stepwise in the above example, only variables that meet the criteria in the Linear Regression Options dialog box are entered in the equation.

# Nonparametric Tests

The Nonparametric Tests submenu on the Analyze menu provides nonparametric tests for one sample or for two or more paired or independent samples. Nonparametric tests do not require assumptions about the shape of the distributions from which the data originate.

## Chi-Square

The Chi-Square Test procedure is used to test hypotheses about the relative proportion of cases falling into several mutually exclusive groups. You can test the hypothesis that people who participated in the survey occur in the same proportions of gender as the general population (50% males, 50% females).

In this example, you will need to recode the string variable *Gender (gender)* into a numeric variable before you can run the procedure.

▶ From the menus choose:

Transform
  Automatic Recode...

This opens the Automatic Recode dialog box.

**Figure 11-11**
*Automatic Recode dialog box*

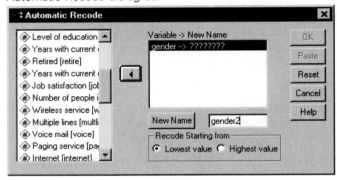

▶ Select the variable *Gender (gender)* and move it to the Variable -> New Name list.

▶ Type gender2 in the New Name text box, and then click the New Name button.

▶ Click OK to run the procedure.

This creates a new numeric variable called *gender2*, which has a value of 1 for females and a value of 2 for males. Now a chi-square test can be run with a numeric variable.

▶ From the menus choose:

Analyze
  Nonparametric Tests
    Chi-Square...

▶ This opens the Chi-Square Test dialog box.

Figure 11-12
*Chi-Square Test dialog box*

▶ Select *Gender (gender2)* as the test variable.

▶ Select All categories equal, since, in the general population of working age, the number of males and females is approximately equal.

▶ Click OK to run the procedure.

The output shows a table of the expected and residual values for the categories. The significance of the chi-square test is 0.6. Consult a statistics or data analysis text book for more information on interpretation of the statistics.

# Time Series Analysis

A time series variable is a variable whose values are recorded at regular intervals over a period of time. The Time Series submenu on the Analyze menu provides exponential smoothing that can be used for predictions. Exponential Smoothing is available in the Student Version and in the Trends module.

## Exponential Smoothing

The Exponential Smoothing procedure performs exponential smoothing of time series data. It creates new series containing predicted values and residuals. This topic uses the *Inventor.sav* file.

For example, you can fit a model for inventory data and use it to predict the next week's inventory. Suppose that for 70 days you have kept track of the inventory of power supplies and that you want to construct a model and then use it to forecast power supplies for the next week.

To use the Exponential Smoothing procedure to forecast power supplies, follow these steps:

▶ Open the *Inventor.sav* file. It is usually in the directory where SPSS is installed.

▶ From the menus choose:

Analyze
  Time Series
    Exponential Smoothing...

This opens the Exponential Smoothing dialog box.

Figure 11-13
*Exponential Smoothing dialog box*

▶ Select *Number of power supplies (amount)* and move it to the Variables list.

▶ Click Parameters to specify the procedure.

This opens the Exponential Smoothing Parameters dialog box.

**Figure 11-14**
*Exponential Smoothing Parameters dialog box*

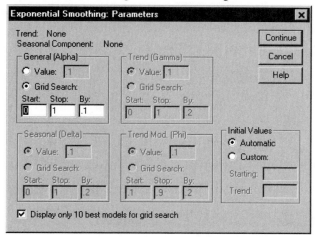

▶ To search for the best general parameter, select Grid Search and then click Continue.

▶ To create a new variable that contains predicted values, click Save.

This opens the Exponential Smoothing Save dialog box.

**Figure 11-15**
*Exponential Smoothing Save dialog box*

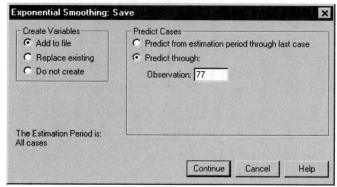

▶ Select Predict through and type 77 in the Observation text box.

This adds 7 days to the original 70.

▶ Click Continue and then in the main dialog box, click OK.

This runs the procedure and adds the new variables *fit_1* and *err_1*. The variable *fit_1* contains the fitted values and the seven new predicted values. The variable *err_1* contains residual values for the original 70 cases; you can use the residuals for further analysis. If you want to save the new variables, select Save As from the File menu and save the data file under a new name.

▶ To see a chart of the original data and the new fit line, from the menus choose:

Graphs
  Sequence...

This opens the Sequence Charts dialog box.

**Figure 11-16**
*Sequence Charts dialog box*

▶ Select *Number of power supplies (amount)* and *Fit for AMOUNT (fit_1)* and move them to the Variables list.

▶ Click OK to run the procedure.

The resulting chart shows both the actual number of power supplies and the fit line plotted on the same axes. The predicted values are plotted for the next week on the right side of the chart.

# IMPORTANT: PLEASE READ THIS INSTALLATION INFORMATION

Dear SPSS 13.0 Graduate Pack Customer,

This package contains your software from SPSS Inc. As part of the installation process, you will be asked for an authorization code to activate the software. If you re-install the software, you will need to re-use this authorization code. Please keep it in a safe place. Your unique authorization code appears below.

If you need support during the installation of your software, many commonly asked questions are answered in the SPSS Resolution Search at **http://support.spss.com**. If you need to contact SPSS Technical Support, information is available on our Web site, **http://support.spss.com**. From there, select "Contact Us."

Thank you for your support of SPSS products and services.

Your authorization code is:

**632a56f444f8670d7918**

# *Index*

Buckles, Bronze
Ogden Leather Design
  130 N. Taylor Street
  Washington, New Jersey 07882

Buckles by Bernard Kelley
The Buckle Works
  Falmouth Avenue
  Santuit, Massachusetts 02635

Clips, Key Case Parts, "D" Rings, Ornaments
Handy Ormond Mfg. Co., Inc.
  50–05 47th Avenue
  Woodside, New York 11377

Eyelets, Rivets, Fasteners, Corners, etc.
Edwin B. Stimpson Co., Inc.
  1515 S.W. 13th Court
  Pompano Beach, Florida 33060

D. D. Holiday & Co.
  15 St. George Street
  St. Augustine, Florida 32084

## Knives

Allied Shoe Machinery Corp.
  241 Winter Street
  Haverhill, Massachusetts 01830

C. S. Osborne Tool Co.
  125 Jersey Street
  Harrison, New Jersey 07029

Worth Leather Co.
  151 Allen Boulevard
  East Farmingdale, New York 11735

X-Acto Precision Tools, Inc.
  48–41 Van Dam Street
  Long Island City, New York 11101

## Last Blocks and Lasts

Century Last Co., Inc.
  1831 10th Street
  Portsmouth, Ohio 45662

Leader Last Co.
  35 Congress Street
  Salem, Massachusetts 01970

S. H. Stafford & Sons
  Morrisville, Vermont 05661

## Leather

A very detailed directory that supplies names of tanners and their specialties is available from:

"Directory of U.S. Leather Tanners"
Tanners' Council of America
  411 Fifth Avenue
  New York, New York 10016

The following are some companies who will sell in small quantities:

A. C. Products
  422 Hudson Street
  New York, New York 10001

Amber Leather Co.
  835 San Julian
  Los Angeles, California 90052

Berman Leather Co.
  147 South Street
  Boston, Massachusetts 02111

Caldwell Lace Leather Co.
  Auburn, Kentucky 42206

Eastern Cut Sole Corp.
  268–274 Broad Street
  Lynn, Massachusetts 01901

J. P. Fliegel Co.
  P.O. Box 505
  Gloversville, New York 12078

A. L. Gebhardt Co.
  226 N. Water Street
  Milwaukee, Wisconsin 53201

D. D. Holiday & Co.
  15 St. George Street
  St. Augustine, Florida 32084

Charles Horowitz & Sons, Inc.
  25 Great Jones Street
  New York, New York 10014

Everything for the leather craftsman from beginner to professional.

Janice Leather Imports, Ltd.
  64 West 23rd Street
  New York, New York 10010

Saks Arts and Crafts
  207 N. Milwaukee Street
  Milwaukee, Wisconsin 53202

M. Siegel Co., Inc.
  114 South Street
  Boston, Massachusetts 02111

Sirois Leather, Inc.
  73 Lowell Street
  Peabody, Massachusetts 01960

Tandy Leather Company Stores

Worth Leather Co.
  151 Allen Boulevard
  East Farmingdale, New York 11735

## Machinery

### Clicking

Allied Shoe Machinery Corp.
  241 Winter Street
  Haverhill, Massachusetts 01830

Handy Ormond Mfg. Co., Inc.
  50–05 47th Avenue
  Woodside, New York 11377

### Needles

Compo Industries, Inc.
  125 Roberts Road
  Waltham, Massachusetts 02154

International Needle Corp.
  1841 Broadway
  New York, New York 10023

Osborne, Tandy, Saks Arts & Crafts, etc.

### Pattern "Paper"

Scorasculpture
Dennison Mfg. Co.
  Framingham, Massachusetts 01701

### Sewing Machinery

Allied Shoe Machinery Corp.
  241 Winter Street
  Haverhill, Massachusetts 01830

Eastern Sewing Machine Co.
  120–124 West 25th Street
  New York, New York 10001

The Singer Co.
  30 Rockefeller Plaza
  New York, New York 10020

United Shoe Machinery Corp.
  140 Federal Street
  Boston, Massachusetts 02110

### Skiving Machinery

Wilcox & Gibbs
  1040 Avenue of the Americas
  New York, New York 10018

### Shears

Compo Industries, Inc.
  125 Roberts Road
  Waltham, Massachusetts 02154

C. S. Osborne Co.
  125 Jersey Street
  Harrison, New Jersey 07029

Henry Westpfal & Co., Inc.
  4 East 32nd Street
  New York, New York 10016

## Tanning Materials

Home Tanning Kits in two sizes, available at
  Tandy Leather Stores.

## Thread

Advance Silk Thread Corp.
  Lodi Street
  Hackensack, New Jersey 07601

American Thread Co.
  90 Park Avenue
  New York, New York 10016

Coats & Clark
  430 Park Avenue
  New York, New York 10022

Premier Thread Co.
  Bristol, Rhode Island 02809

Waxed Threads
M. Rossi & Son
  401 S. Clinton Avenue
  Trenton, New Jersey 08609

## Tools

All Craft Tool & Supply Co.
  215 Park Avenue
  Hicksville, Long Island, New York 11801

Anchor Tool & Supply Co.
  12 John Street
  New York, New York 10038

Dick Blick
  P.O. Box 1267
  Galesburg, Illinois 61401

CCM : Arts & Crafts, Inc.
9520 Baltimore Avenue
College Park, Maryland 20740

Economy Handicrafts, Inc.
47–11 Francis Lewis Boulevard
Flushing, New York 11361

D. D. Holiday & Co.
100 Carver Street
St. Augustine, Florida 32084

C. S. Osborne Tool Co.
125 Jersey Street
Harrison, New Jersey 07029

Saks Arts & Crafts
207 N. Milwaukee Street
Milwaukee, Wisconsin 53202

Tandy Leather Company Stores

United Shoe Machinery
104 Federal Street
Boston, Massachusetts 02109

Henry Westpfal & Co., Inc.
4 East 32nd Street
New York, New York 10016

Worth Leather Co.
151 Allen Boulevard
East Farmingdale, New York 11735

### Waxes, Preservatives, and Polishes

Shoemakers, department stores, and sports shops sell a variety of leather preservatives, including Lexol, neat's-foot oil, and saddle soaps.

Dubbin
Tana Co. of America, Inc.
Elmsford, New York 10523

Mel-O-Wax
Wynnewood, Pennsylvania 19096

Mermac Mink Oil Mfg. Co.
2625 Salem-Dallas Highway
Salem, Oregon 97308

Prime Neat's-Foot Compound
Dominion Chemical Co.
Puddledock Road
Petersburg, Virginia 23803

# Index

*Page numbers in italics refer to illustrations.*